Let's Hear It for the

Fruit of the Spirit!

12 Instant Bible Lessons for Kids

Edited by Lois Keffer and Mary Grace Becker

NEXGEN®

Building the New Generation of Believers

An Imprint of Cook Communications Ministries
COLORADO SPRINGS, COLORADO • PARIS, ONTARIO
KINGSWAY COMMUNICATIONS, LTD., EASTBOURNE, ENGLAND

Pick Up 'n' Do: Let's Hear It for the Fruit of the Spirit!
Copyright © 2005 Cook Communications Ministries

Scripture quotations, unless otherwise noted, are from

Edited by: Mary Grace Becker, Lois Keffer
Written by: Debbie Allmon, Mary Grace Becker, Kathleen Dowdy, Kim Gunderson, Susan Epperson, Dana Hood, Lindy Keffer, Lois Keffer, Susan Martins Miller, Faye Spieker, Susan Vannaman, Jennifer Wilger, Paula Yingst
Art Direction: Nancy L. Haskins
Cover Design: Helen Harrison
Interior Design: Helen Harrison, Nancy L. Haskins, Lois Keffer
Illustrators: Kris and Sharon Cartwright and Lois Keffer

Printed in the United States

First printing, 2005
1 2 3 4 5 6 7 8 9 10   09 08 07 06 05

ISBN 0781440661

Table of Contents

Quick Start Guide **4**

Lesson 1   **Help on the Way** **7**
John 14:15–18, 26, 27; 15:8, 11–17

Lesson 2   **The Holy Spirit Comes at Pentecost** **17**
Acts 1:4, 5, 8; 2:1–6, 14, 22–24, 37, 38, 41

Lesson 3   **For Goodness' Sake!** **27**
Acts 2:42–47; 4:32–37

Lesson 4   **Jump, Shout, Knock Yourself Out!** **37**
Acts 3:1–16

Lesson 5   **Courage Under Fire** **47**
Acts 4:1–13

Lesson 6   **Ananias in Action** **57**
Acts 9:1–18

Lesson 7   **Barnabas at Bat** **67**
Acts 9:19–31

Lesson 8   **Peter Escapes from Prison** **77**
Acts 12:6–18

Lesson 9   **Crowd Control** **87**
Acts 14:8–18

Lesson 10   **Home Away from Home** **97**
Acts 16:11–15

Lesson 11   **Jailhouse Rock** **107**
Acts 16:16–19, 23, 25–34

Lesson 12   **The Chariot Chase** **117**
Acts 8:4–6, 26–39

Quick Start Guide

Pick Up 'n' Do! elementary lessons give your kids great Bible teaching and serious discipleship without hours of preparation. You and your kids will love these large group/small group lessons. Two options let you take the lesson from super simple to more challenging.

If you're looking for an "instant" lesson that you can pick up and do at the last minute, you've got it in Bible 4U! and Shepherd's Spot.

All you need is a photocopier and basic classroom supplies such as pencils, scissors and glue sticks. Copy the **Bible 4U!** instant drama and the **Shepherd's Spot** handout and you're ready to go.

Are you looking for something beyond the basics?

The optional **Get Set** section of the lessons gives you an opportunity to get a puppet into the action. "Schooner" is a mouthy macaw whose bright remarks will bring giggles and grins each week. And he does a smack-up job of setting up the Bible story.

Don't have a puppet ministry team in your church? How about recruiting middle schoolers? The lively back and forth between Schooner and the Leader is right up their alley. What a great way to get them involved in ministry to younger children!

Now for the heart of the lesson

Bible 4U!

The Bible is full of drama! What better way to teach than with fascinating dramas that take a unique approach to each Bible story? Photocopy the instant drama, pull volunteers from your group to read the roles and you're ready to go.

You'll keep your knowledgeable students engaged, and give kids who are new to God's Word a solid foundation of biblical truth. The dramas call for just a few characters. You may want to play the main role yourself. Or, call on a teen or adult drama troupe to prepare and present the dramas each week. Either way, kids will see the Bible stories come to life in unforgettable ways.

Shepherd's Spot

This is the second essential step of the lesson. After **Bible 4U!**, kids break into small groups with one adult helper for every eight to ten kids. Nothing leaves a more indelible impact on kids' lives than the warm, personal touch of a caring adult. The photocopiable instructions and handouts will give your helpers the confidence they need to help kids consider how to live out what they've learned.

In the **Shepherd's Spot**, kids will read the story straight from the Bible. They'll learn basic Bible skills and complete a fun, photocopiable handout that helps them understand how to get the story off the page and into their lives. They'll close each week by sharing concerns and praying together.

Workshop Wonders

And there's more! Each week, the optional **Workshop Wonders** section gives you a game, craft, science or cooking activity that gets your kids out of their chairs and into the action.

The **Workshop Wonders** activities require more than the usual classroom supplies. If you choose one of these activities, you'll need to pick up cooking or science ingredients or a few simple craft or game supplies. If you don't mind a little extra preparation, you'll find that there's nothing like a little hands-on action to bring that moment of learning wonder to kids' faces.

These special activities are guaranteed to make a memory and help the Bible lesson stick with kids for a long time to come.

That's it! You can go for a quick, simple lesson with **Bible 4U!** and the **Shepherd's Spot**.

If you wish, add another level of excitement and learning with the Schooner script in the optional **Get Set** section of each lesson.

And if you love teaching with activities, do a little shopping and give kids the memorable experiences of **Workshop Wonders**.

Do you want to give your kids even more great stuff?

How About Staff?

Finding Schooner

If you do the **Get Set** option to open the lessons, you'll need to purchase a parrot or scarlet macaw puppet.

You'll find a great selection on the Internet, in all sizes and prices. Type "scarlet macaw puppet" into your favorite search engine and browse until you find the puppet that suits your price range.

You need just a few helpers to make Pick Up 'n' Do lessons a great experience for you and your kids!

1. A leader/emcee hosts the **Bible 4U!** instant drama each week. For a quick presentation, pull kids from your group to read the roles in the dramas. When there are just one or two parts, you may want to step into the leading role yourself.

2. You may wish to ask a small drama troupe to prepare the stories each week. Five or six volunteers who serve on a rotating basis can easily cover the stories with just a few minutes' preparation.

3. For the **Shepherd's Spot**, you'll need one adult leader for every eight to ten kids. You'll need caring adults in this role—people who are good listeners and feel comfortable sharing their lives with kids. This is a great first step into children's ministry for adults who haven't taught before.

4. If you choose to do the optional **Get Set** puppet script, you'll need a leader and a puppeteer. It's best to use the same leader who hosts the Bible dramas. If you recruit a couple of people to play Schooner, they can rotate every few weeks.

For Overachievers

Do you have a great stage set-up at your church? Then you may want to go for some flash and glitz. Give Schooner a little tropical cabana with a palm tree and a sea-breezy backdrop. Make sure your leader has an obnoxious tropical shirt to slip on.

Don't forget the music! Warm kids up each week with lively, interactive praise songs. Then bring on Schooner's set to the tune of island rhythms.

Equip your drama troupe with a box full of Bibletime costumes. You'll find tips for props and staging in the "for Overachievers" box just before each Bible story. Of course, all this pizzazz is purely optional. The most important ingredient in a wonderful Bible lesson is YOU—the warm, caring leader whose love for kids calls you into children's ministry in the first place! There is absolutely no substitute for the personal attention you give to children each week. You become the model of Jesus himself through your gifts of time and commitment.

God bless you as you minister to his kids!

Help on the Way

Get Set
Option

LARGE GROUP ■ Greet kids and do a puppet skit. Schooner learns new and wonderful things about the Holy Spirit.

❑ large bird puppet   ❑ puppeteer

Bible 4U! Instant Drama
1

LARGE GROUP ■ Dropped balls emphasize the missed opportunities to welcome the Holy Spirit into our hearts.

❑ 4 actors ❑ copies of pp. 10-11, Last-Minute Instructions script ❑ Bible ❑ 4 crumpled paper balls ❑ 2 construction paper hearts ❑ simple drawing of a house ❑ 4 numbered balls Optional: ❑ 4 white balloons ❑ white crepe paper streamers ❑ bag to hold props

Shepherd's Spot
2

SMALL GROUP ■ Use "The Gift Jesus Promised" handout to introduce kids to the ways God's Holy Spirit works in our lives.

❑ Bibles ❑ pencils ❑ scissors ❑ glue sticks ❑ copies of p. 14, The Gift Jesus Promised ❑ copies of p. 16, Special Delivery

Workshop Wonders
Option

SMALL GROUP ■ Learn the value of a guide as kids construct and negotiate a challenging obstacle course.

❑ brightly-colored yarn ❑ box of treats ❑ toys and furniture to create an obstacle course ❑ blindfolds

Bible Basis
Jesus promises a Counselor.
John 14:15–18, 26, 27; 15:8, 11–17

Learn It!
Jesus promised the Holy Spirit would help us.

Live It!
Live in God's power.

Bible Verse
I will ask the Father, and he will give you another Counselor to be with you forever—the Spirit of truth.
John 14:16, 17

Quick Takes

John 14:15–18, 26, 27; 15:8, 11–17

14:15 "If you love me, you will obey what I command.

16 And I will ask the Father, and he will give you another Counselor to be with you for ever-17 the Spirit of truth. The world cannot accept him, because it neither sees him nor knows him. But you know him, for he lives with you and will be in you.

18 I will not leave you as orphans; I will come to you.

26 But the Counselor, the Holy Spirit, whom the Father will send in my name, will teach you all things and will remind you of everything I have said to you.

27 Peace I leave with you; my peace I give you. I do not give to you as the world gives. Do not let your hearts be troubled and do not be afraid."

15:8 This is to my Father's glory, that you bear much fruit, showing yourselves to be my disciples.

11 I have told you this so that my joy may be in you and that your joy may be complete.

12 My command is this: Love each other as I have loved you.

13 Greater love has no one than this, that he lay down his life for his friends.

14 You are my friends if you do what I command.

15 I no longer call you servants, because a servant does not know his master's business. Instead, I have called you friends, for everything that I learned from my Father I have made known to you.

16 You did not choose me, but I chose you and appointed you to go and bear fruit—fruit that will last. Then the Father will give you whatever you ask in my name.

17 This is my command: Love each other."

Insights

When Jesus first mentioned the coming of the Holy Spirit, the disciples probably felt a bit clueless. Why would they need a counselor and helper when the Son of God was with them? The conversation was frightening for the little group of 12 who had so faithfully followed their beloved rabbi for nearly three years.

The setting was the upper room where Jesus celebrated the Last Supper. Jesus seemed intense and a bit sad. He knew his work on earth was nearly done. He knew the suffering that lay before him, and that these dear friends who surrounded him would desert him in his most terrible hour. He was well aware of the confusion and despair they'd feel as he died on the cross. They would be lost without him. So he prepared them by promising that he would not leave them alone.

You have to wonder how much of this wonderful teaching about the coming of the Holy Spirit the disciples grasped. Jesus promised to send a Counselor, the Spirit of truth, who would live with them and be in them. He would teach them all things and remind them of everything Jesus had taught. This incredible gift from God would serve as an internal spiritual guidance system to those who were left on earth to do God's work.

And, oh, do kids ever need God's internal guidance system in their lives today! As they face the challenge of living for God in a postmodern society, the Holy Spirit whispers God's truth. As acts of terrorism play out on their TV screens, God gently promises never to leave them alone. Use this lesson to help kids grasp the wonderful gift Jesus promised to his faithful followers, the gift of the Holy Spirit.

Get Set

Open with lively music, then greet the kids. **Hello! Gather around, everyone, and let's hear about living with God's power. Jesus promised his friends a helper when he left them to live with his Father in heaven. I need a really smart parrot to help me with today's Holy Spirit story.** *Schooner hides behind the Leader or behind the Leader's chair.*

Schooner: *Squawk!*

Leader: I hear you, Schooner.

Schooner: Squawk!

Leader: *(searches the group)* But I can't see you.

Schooner: *(pops up)* Boo!

Leader: There you are!

Schooner: You said spirit, so I thought I'd pretend to be a ghost.

Leader: We're going to talk about the Holy Spirit today.

Schooner: *Eeek! (ducks head in wing)* Sounds spooky, boss.

Leader: The Holy Spirit is not someone to be scared of.

Schooner: *(peeks out)* No?

Leader: No.

Schooner: The Holy Spirit is friendly?

Leader: Much more than friendly. He's loving and powerful. God sends the Holy Spirit to be with people who love Jesus.

Schooner: The Holy Spirit is from God?

Leader: Sure is. The Holy Spirit is a friend who is always with us, teaching us God's truth and reminding us of what Jesus wants us to do.

Schooner: Does everybody need reminding as much as I do, boss?

Leader: We all need to be reminded of what Jesus taught. That's why Jesus promised his disciples that a helper would come.

Schooner: But that was a long time ago.

Leader: Jesus promises us the same thing.

Schooner: And the children here?

Leader: Ditto.

Schooner: You mean the Holy Spirit can be their helper too?

Leader: Always. Every day.

Schooner: Wow.

Leader: Jesus said if we obey him and keep on thinking about what he taught us, he will send the Holy Spirit to be our guide.

Schooner: *(pauses a moment)* But we can't see him?

Leader: Nope.

Schooner: *(nods head slowly)* Then how do we know he's there?

Leader: We open our hearts to God, Schooner.

Schooner: And he, like, talks to us?

Leader: It's like having a little voice inside, teaching us what is right. And he's always with us.

Schooner: So we're never alone.

Leader: Right. The Holy Spirit is there to comfort and help. Jesus said, "I will ask the Father, and he will give you another Counselor to be with you forever."

Schooner: *(leans on the Leader)* Forever! I like the sound of that.

Leader: You'll like this, too. The Holy Spirit brings us love and joy and peace and lots of other good things.

Schooner: *(sighs)* That makes me feel all warm and fuzzy inside, boss *(drops his head on Leader's shoulder and snores loudly)*

Leader: A parrot snoring on my shoulder! Who would have guessed?

Schooner: *(Zzzzzzz. Zzzzzzz)*

Leader: *(whispers)* Live in God's power. Jesus is closer than you think!

Schooner: *(mumbles, dreamlike)* Bible 4U! up next...*zzzzzzz*

1 Bible 4U!

Have you heard last-minute instructions like this before? "To bed and lights out by ten o'clock, don't touch the pie that's in the fridge and don't let the dogs out." When your parents plan to go out and ask someone else to take care of you, they prepare big time. They let the childsitter know where things are and make sure to pass on emergency phone numbers. And they tell you about who's coming to take care of you.

Jesus gave last-minute instructions to his disciples. He knew he was about to go to the cross. He would die, then he would rise again and go to heaven. The disciples wouldn't be able to see him or touch him. But Jesus wasn't going to leave them alone. He was sending the Holy Spirit to stay with them, comfort them and guide them in God's truth. Today we're going to hear Jesus' very words as he gave the disciples last-minute instructions about the Holy Spirit who would come and never leave them.

We have guests who will help us understand what Jesus said about the Holy Spirit. Let's welcome Max, a follower of Jesus. *(Max enters and stands off to one side.)* Now welcome Lou and Stella. *(They enter and stand on the opposite side.)* See if you can discover what's important to Lou and Stella.

Instant Prep
Choose a Narrator, or play that part yourself. Choose three volunteers to be Max (or Maxine), Lou and Stella. Give them copies of the "Last Minute Instructions" script. You'll need four balls of crumpled white paper, two paper hearts, a Bible, and a simple drawing of a house.

for Overachievers
Ask a four-person drama team to prepare the story. Have them collect the following props: three white balloons with white crepe paper streamers, three hearts, a Bible, a drawing of a house and a bag to hold the props.

Last-Minute Instructions
Based on John 14:15–18, 26, 27; 15:8, 11–17

(Narrator sits at the center on stool with a bag of props. Max sits stage right, holding a small heart. Lou and Stella stand stage left. They mime talking together.)

Narrator: Just before Jesus was arrested, he told his disciples, "If you love me, you will do what I command."

Max nods yes and brings a heart to the Narrator who puts it into the bag. The Narrator looks at Lou and Stella expectantly. They shake their heads and wave the Narrator off.

Narrator: Then I will ask the Father to give you the Spirit of truth, a counselor to be with you forever.

Tosses a paper ball (or balloon with streamers) to Max who catches it, surprised but happy.

Max: A counselor? What kind of counselor?

Narrator: The very Spirit of God! He will live in you and always be with you.

Max: *(holds the paper ball over his heart)* God's Holy Spirit will never leave me?

Narrator: You'll never be alone, Max. Jesus promised to send the Holy Spirit because he wouldn't always be with his followers on earth.

Max: *(holds the paper ball in the air)* Thank you, God, for this wonderful gift. I never, ever want you to leave me alone. Live in me, and teach me how to follow Jesus.

Lou: *(scoffing)* That Max guy is annoying.

Stella: No kidding. He needs to get a life.

Narrator: *(to Lou and Stella)* You'll never know true life until you know Jesus.

Stella: *Puh-leeze!* I like my life fine just the way it is.

Narrator: *(reads from Scripture to the audience)* The world cannot accept him, because they don't see him or know him.

Narrator tosses another paper ball to Lou and Stella. They continue to chat and don't see it. It drops on the floor beside them.

Max: Hey! Hey, you guys pick it up! Look it's right there! *(Lou and Stella look around puzzled, shrug, and go back to chatting)*

Narrator: Jesus said, "If anyone loves me, he will obey my teaching. My Father will love him."

Narrator pulls out a large heart and takes it to Max who hugs it. Lou and Stella notice.

Stella: Hey, I want one of those. Give me one!

Narrator: *(throws another paper ball to them but they don't see it, turns to Max)* My Father will make his home with him.

Narrator pulls a drawing of a house and gives it to Max, who reacts with joy.

Lou: Hey! What about us?

Narrator: *(throws another paper ball but again it is ignored, shakes head and sighs, looks at the script)* Jesus said, "He who does not love

me will not obey my teaching." Do you obey Jesus' teaching?

Stella: Well, no.

Narrator: Sorry. *(shrugs and reads again)* Jesus said, "These aren't my words; they belong to the Father who sent me. All of this I tell you while I am with you but the Holy Spirit, *(Max holds up his paper ball)* whom God the Father will send, will teach you everything." *(gives Max a Bible)*

Max: There's so much I don't know. Like what to do if people *(points a thumb at Lou and Stella)* say I'm a loser. I need God's help when stuff like that happens.

Narrator: That's what the Holy Spirit does for those who put their faith in Jesus. He wants us to have his peace.

Max: *(holds up the heart)* I can't think of anything better than peace in my heart.

Narrator: Jesus said, "You did not choose me, but I chose you and appointed you to go and bear fruit—fruit that will last."

Max, Lou, Stella: Fruit?

Lou: What—does God want us to be trees or something?

Narrator: Jesus explained that if we obey him we'll remain in his love and God will bring good things from our lives.

Lou: Good things like having gobs of money and being popular?

Narrator: Good things like love and joy and peace.

Stella: And is all this stuff, like, free?

Narrator: Jesus paid for it with his life. That's how much he loves you. Put your faith in him, and he'll send the Holy Spirit to be your helper and friend.

They exit.

Isn't that awesome? Jesus knew he was returning to heaven, so he promised to send the Holy Spirit to be with us always. Let's see what you understood about God's Holy Spirit from this story.

Toss the four numbered balls to different parts of the room. Bring kids with the balls to the front one-by-one and ask these questions. Allow kids to get help from the group if they need it. After each correct answer, let kids drop their balls into a bag.

 ■ **Why did Jesus promise to send the Holy Spirit?**

 ■ **What did Jesus ask us to do?**

 ■ **What did Jesus say the Holy Spirit would do for people who believe in him and follow him?**

 ■ **Why do we need God's Holy Spirit in our lives?**

The disciples probably wanted to keep Jesus with them for their whole lives. No one else could do the things Jesus did. He healed sick people and he told about God's love in ways no one had ever done before. Jesus was their teacher, their rabbi, and they lived with him and traveled with him wherever he went. But Jesus knew he was about to be arrested. Jesus dying on the cross so our sins can be forgiven was part of God's plan.

Bible Verse
I will ask the Father, and he will give you another Counselor to be with you forever—the Spirit of truth. John 14:16, 17

Jesus wanted his followers—both in Bible times and today— to know that he wasn't leaving them alone. He promised to send the Holy Spirit to live in our hearts, to guide us and comfort us every day. When we give our lives to Jesus and obey the things he taught, the Holy Spirit is like a voice whispering in our hearts, teaching us and reminding us of God's truth.

When the Holy Spirit is at work in our lives, he makes wonderful things happen. He gives us love, joy and peace—and lots of other things that we'll learn about in the weeks to come.

Today in your shepherd groups, you'll make a reminder of the gift of the Holy Spirit that Jesus promised to send his followers.

Dismiss kids to their shepherd groups.

2 Shepherd's Spot

Gather your small group and help kids find John 14 in their Bibles.

John is the fourth book in the New Testament. The four gospels, Matthew, Mark, Luke and John, tell about the life of Jesus on earth. What we heard today happened near the end of Jesus' life. He shared a meal with his disciples and told them about the Holy Spirit who would come to be their helper. Let's read what Jesus said straight from God's Word.

Have volunteers take turns reading John 14:15–18, 26, 27, 15:8, 11–17 aloud.

■ **Is there someone you know who always gives you good advice? Tell about that person.**

Most of us have people we can trust—people who help us figure out the right thing to do. But people can't always be with us. Even Jesus was only with a few people at a time. So when Jesus went back to heaven, God sent the Holy Spirit to be our guide. The Holy Spirit is an amazing gift from God for people who love Jesus with all their hearts. This little gift box will help us understand more about God's gift of the Holy Spirit.

Distribute "The Gift Jesus Promised," p. 14. Show kids how to cut out and fold the box.

■ **If we love and obey Jesus, how will the Holy Spirit help us?** *(He'll be our helper and friend: never leave us alone; guide us into God's truth; remind us of what Jesus said.)*

Write a few words inside your gift box that will remind you of how God's Holy Spirit can work in your life. This would be an opportune moment to invite kids who've never given their lives to Jesus to do so.

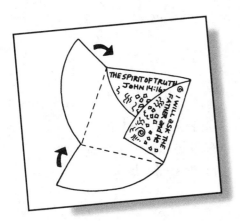

■ **Do you have any questions about the Holy Spirit?** Take this opportunity to explain your church's specific teachings on the Holy Spirit.

God's spirit can be with us all the time. Not just when we're in church, but in school, at home, in a crowd of people and when we're alone. And the Holy Spirit is with us when we pray. Invite kids to share their concerns, then close with prayer. **Dear Lord, thank you for teaching us about all the wonderful things the Holy Spirit does in the hearts of people who believe in you. Today we pray for (mention each child's concerns). We pray that your spirit will guide us this week. In Jesus name, amen.**

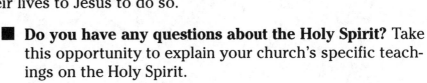

THE GIFT JESUS PROMISED

Make this folded box as a reminder of the gift Jesus promised to send his followers—the gift of the Holy Spirit.

1. Cut out the shape on the dark lines.
2. Write your name in the blank on the flap.
3. Inside the box, write different ways the Holy Spirit helps those who love Jesus.

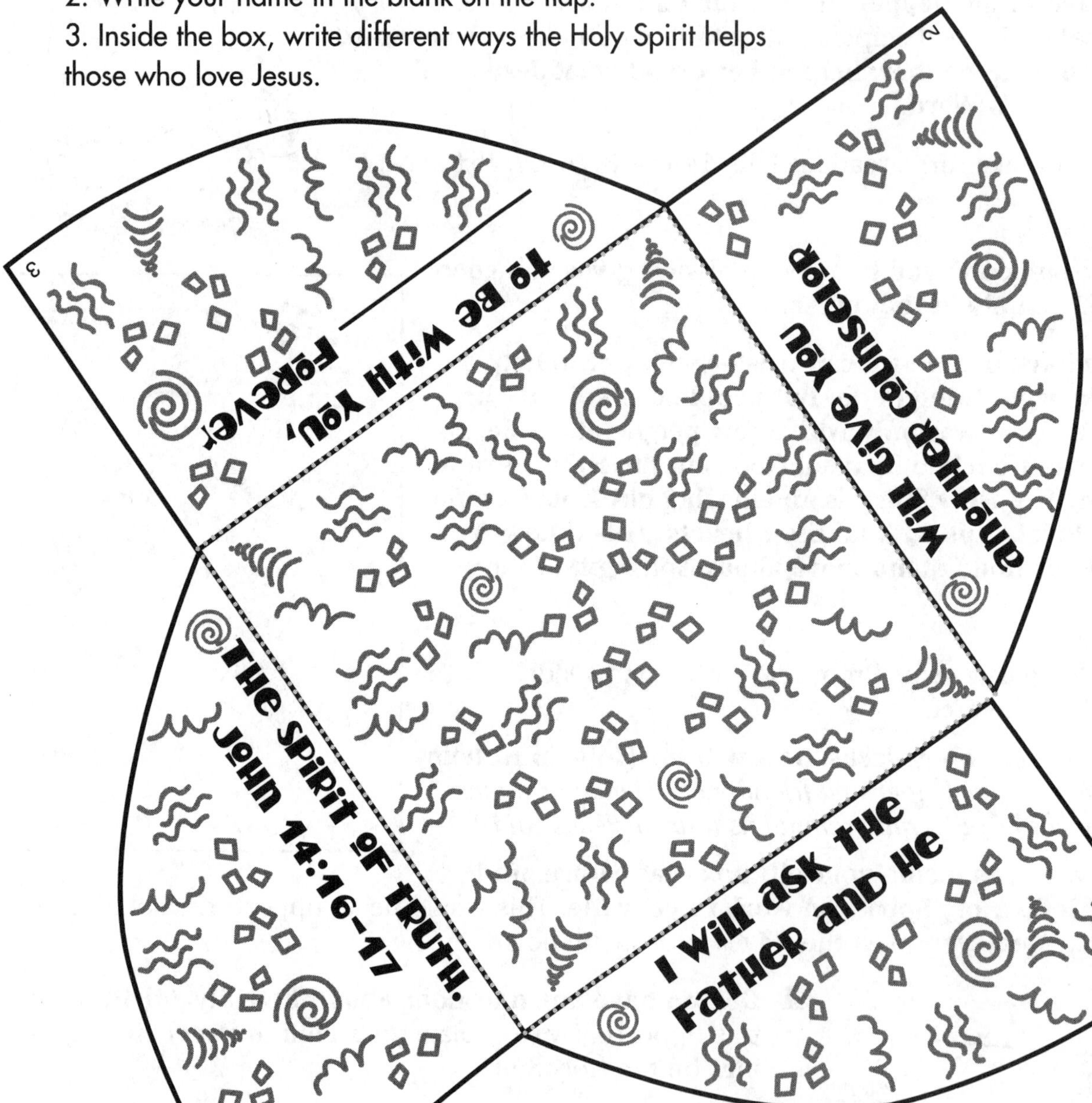

To be with you, forever.'

another Counselor

Will give you

The Spirit of truth.
John 14:16–17

I will ask the Father and He

4. Fold in flaps 1 through 4 on the dotted lines.
5. Tuck flap 4 under flap 1 to close the box.

14

Workshop Wonders

Gather props to build an obstacle course. Cover tables to make tunnels. Use clean wastebaskets, chairs, piles of books, crates and other items from your teaching space. You may want to enlist older kids to help you build a safe but challenging course. Mark a path through the course with brightly colored yarn. Place a box of treats at the end of the course.

■ **Have you ever been on an amusement park ride that was both scary and exciting? What was that like?**

■ **What about an adventure? Did you have a guide? What did that person do?**

Every day of our lives is a new adventure. When the sun rises in the morning, we never know what new challenges the day may bring. But we do know this—Jesus promised that when we trust in him, the Holy Spirit will be our counselor and guide. So we don't need to be afraid of anything that comes our way. The Holy Spirit will be with us, reminding us of what Jesus taught.

You're each going to need a guide to make it through this obstacle course to the sweet reward at the end.

Have kids form pairs. Let kids decide which will be the Traveler and which will be the Guide. Blindfold the Traveler.

Here are the rules. The Guide cannot touch the Traveler. The Guide's job is to talk the Traveler through the course. Only the Guide can talk. Everyone else needs to keep quiet so the Traveler can hear the Guide's instructions. Quiet in the house, please!

Let a new pair start through the obstacle course when the first pair is halfway through. When everyone has gone through the course, change it slightly. Then have the Travelers and Guides reverse roles.

Gather everyone in a circle and the let them enjoy their treats.

■ **Which did you like best—being the Traveler or the Guide? Why?**

■ **How was the obstacle course like a day in your life?**

■ **How is the Holy Spirit the best guide you could ever have?**

I noticed that you really paid attention to your Guides as you worked through the obstacle course. This week I hope you'll pay attention to the Holy Spirit—he's always there to teach and guide you.

Fold down the corners to start your paper airplane.

SPECIAL DELIVERY

TO

Live in God's power.

Today at church we learned that Jesus promised his followers the help of the Holy Spirit. « Why would the disciples need the help of the Holy Spirit once Jesus left them? » Why is it great to know that you can count on the Holy Spirit to be with you?

The Holy Spirit is our helper. Grab a helper to play this fun little game. Pick a favorite song. Hum it a few times to get the words in your head. Then sing the song with your helper with you taking the first word and he or she the second and so on. Try not to sing the same word twice but do try to sing the whole song without skipping a beat!

Bible Verse

I will ask the Father, and he will give you another Counselor to be with you forever— the Spirit of truth. John 14:16, 17

◇ If you could put a face on the Holy Spirit, what would he look like?

◇ Does the Holy Spirit take lunch breaks or go on vacation? In other words, is the Holy Spirit always there to help? Why or why not?

Family FUN

Live It!

The Holy Spirit Comes at Pentecost

Option N

Get Set

LARGE GROUP ■ Greet kids and do a puppet skit. Schooner learns what happened on the day of Pentecost.

❑ *large bird puppet*   ❑ *puppeteer*

1

Bible 4U! Instant Drama

LARGE GROUP ■ Three birds tell how they were "blown away" when God sent the Holy Spirit to empower Jesus' followers at Pentecost.

❑ *4 actors* ❑ *copies of pp. 20-21, Blow, Spirit, Blow script* ❑ *4 numbered balls*
Optional: ❑ *Bibletime costume* ❑ *brightly colored sweatpants and tops* ❑ *feather boas* ❑ *3 stools* ❑ *fan*

2

Shepherd's Spot

SMALL GROUP ■ Use the "Wind of the Spirit" handout to help kids realize that God's power is at work in the lives of those who obey him.

❑ *Bibles* ❑ *pencils* ❑ *scissors* ❑ *glue sticks* ❑ *paper clips* ❑ *copies of p. 24, Wind of the Spirit* ❑ *copies of p. 26, Special Delivery*

Option

Workshop Wonders

SMALL GROUP ■ Make balsa wood racers powered by wind as reminders that the Holy Spirit empowers us for God's work.

❑ *lightweight balsa wood* ❑ *ruler* ❑ *cardboard* ❑ *patterns for 1-inch circles* ❑ *8 or 10-inch balloons* ❑ *plastic drinking straws* ❑ *masking tape* ❑ *wood glue* ❑ *push pins* ❑ *scissors Optional:* ❑ *hot glue gun* ❑ *string*

Bible Basis
The Holy Spirit at Pentecost.
Acts 1:4, 5, 8;
2:1–6, 14, 22–24,
37, 38, 41

Learn It!
God's Holy Spirit works through us.

Live It!
Do God's work.

Bible Verse
You will receive power when the Holy Spirit comes on you; and you will be my witnesses. Acts 1:8

Quick Takes

Acts 1:4, 5, 8; 2:1–6, 14, 22–24, 37, 38, 41

1:4 On one occasion, while he was eating with them, he gave them this command: "Do not leave Jerusalem, but wait for the gift my Father promised, which you have heard me speak about.

5 For John baptized with water, but in a few days you will be baptized with the Holy Spirit.

8 But you will receive power when the Holy Spirit comes on you; and you will be my witnesses in Jerusalem, and in all Judea and Samaria, and to the ends of the earth."

2:1 When the day of Pentecost came, they were all together in one place.

2 Suddenly a sound like the blowing of a violent wind came from heaven and filled the whole house where they were sitting.

3 They saw what seemed to be tongues of fire that separated and came to rest on each of them.

4 All of them were filled with the Holy Spirit and began to speak in other tongues as the Spirit enabled them.

5 Now there were staying in Jerusalem God-fearing Jews from every nation under heaven.

6 When they heard this sound, a crowd came together in bewilderment, because each one heard them speaking in his own language.

14 Then Peter stood up with the Eleven, raised his voice and addressed the crowd: "Fellow Jews and all of you who live in Jerusalem, let me explain this to you; listen carefully to what I say.

22 "Men of Israel, listen to this: Jesus of Nazareth was a man accredited by God to you by miracles, wonders and signs, which God did among you through him, as you yourselves know.

23 This man was handed over to you by God's set purpose and foreknowledge; and you, with the help of wicked men, put him to death by nailing him to the cross.

24 But God raised him from the dead, freeing him from the agony of death, because it was impossible for death to keep its hold on him."

37 When the people heard this, they were cut to the heart and said to Peter and the other apostles, "Brothers, what shall we do?"

38 Peter replied, "Repent and be baptized, every one of you, in the name of Jesus Christ for the forgiveness of your sins. And you will receive the gift of the Holy Spirit."

41 Those who accepted his message were baptized, and about three thousand were added to their number that day.

Insights

How often have you thought, "Lord, I'm not quite sure what you're doing here? Could I have a step-by-step plan and a timeline?" You can sense that kind of tension playing through the lines of this story. Jesus' followers didn't expect him to die. His appearances following the resurrection still left them a bit confused. They got up the courage to ask aloud, "Now will you restore the kingdom to Israel?" His response? It's not for you to know God's timing. Wait here. You'll receive power from the Holy Spirit, and then you'll be my witnesses. Then he left them staring on a mountaintop as he returned to heaven.

Having little idea of what to expect or when to expect it, the disciples waited in Jerusalem just as they had been told. And then it happened! The Holy Spirit "blew in" to the room where they were gathered. Flames appeared above the heads of the disciples and soon they spilled into the street proclaiming the Good News with power. People heard the message in their own languages and believed in Jesus by the thousands. Wouldn't that have made the headlines on all the news channels!

Waiting in obedience for God's Spirit to work is challenging for even the most mature believer. Think about how it must feel to kids. *Can I really know what it's like to have God's Spirit in my heart? Will he ever use me to do important stuff?*

Use this lesson to teach kids that we can trust God to come in power when the time is right and that the Holy Spirit will use those who are faithful and obedient in ways we can hardly imagine.

Open with lively music, then greet the kids. **I'm glad to see everyone here today. I'm ready to do God's work—how 'bout you? With the help of the Holy Spirit we can do a lot for God's kingdom right where we live. Schooner, drop in and say hi.** *Schooner pops up.*

Schooner: Excuse me, boss, but did I hear you say drop in?

Leader: I think so.

Schooner: Um. Droppings are not a popular subject with birds.

Leader: Oh?

Schooner: Many a bird has been banished, caged and chased with brooms because of droppings.

Leader: My, my. How about if I just say, "Hello, Schooner"?

Schooner: Much better.

Leader: Hello, Schooner.

Schooner: Yell-ow boss!

Leader: God has work for us to do. And it starts right here where we live.

Schooner: Does this have something to do with today's Bible story?

Leader: Of course! Long ago on a very special day, God sent the Holy Spirit to Jesus' friends.

Schooner: Does this special day have a special name?

Leader: The day of Pentecost.

Schooner: Plenty-cost. Was it expensive?

Leader: Pen-te-cost. And it was filled with excitement!

Schooner: So what was so exciting?

Leader: First of all, a sound like a mighty wind rushed through the room where Jesus' disciples were gathered.

Schooner: I'm not too fond of wind. Makes it difficult to fly.

Leader: This was a wind from heaven. And flames of fire rested on each of the people there.

Schooner: *Squawk!* Once I got too close to a fire and my feathers got singed.

Leader: This fire was a sign from God, Schooner. The wind and fire meant that God was doing something very special.

Schooner: I'll say. So what happened next?

Leader: The disciples were filled with the Holy Spirit. They went right out into the street and started telling everyone about Jesus in all kinds of different languages.

Schooner: I speak different languages, boss.

Leader: You're full of surprises, Schooner. What languages do you speak?

Schooner: I speak chickadee, pigeon and a little North American barn swallow.

Leader: Really? I thought you just squawked. Anyway, when the disciples told about Jesus, thousands of people believed in him that very day.

Schooner: Wow. How could that happen?

Leader: By the power of God's Holy Spirit.

Schooner: So where do I sign up to get this power?

Leader: The Holy Spirit comes to people who love Jesus.

Schooner: Hmm. People way back then when Jesus lived. How nice for them.

Leader: Way back then and people today. The Holy Spirit is God's gift to his people to help them do his work.

Schooner: You mean, somebody in this very room might do something important for God?

Leader: That's right. His power never runs out!

Schooner: I gotta' hear more about this.

Leader: You're about to. Guess who's doing the Bible story today.

Schooner: Gimme a hint.

Leader: They have wings and feathers and they fly up high in the sky.

Schooner: Birds? We're gonna have birds in Bible 4U!? Well, come on—let's go, go, go, there right now, now, now! *Squawk!*

① Bible 4U!

Welcome to Bible 4U! Today we're going to hear how Jesus sent the Holy Spirit to help his followers. Anybody know anything about the Holy Spirit? Let kids respond, then continue: **Just before Jesus went back to heaven, he promised his followers that the Holy Spirit would come to be with them and help them do God's work. With the Holy Spirit's help, they'd be able to spread the good news about Jesus all around Jerusalem, to nearby cities and towns, and all around the world!**

Instant Prep

Before class, assign kids to play Dilbert Dove, Doris Dove, Perry Pigeon and Peter. Give them copies of the "Blow, Spirit, Blow" script below.

Jesus' followers were excited about the coming of the Holy Spirit, but they probably had a lot of questions. Would the Holy Spirit be a person like Jesus? Would they be able to see him? How would they know when the Holy Spirit came? Even though they didn't know exactly what to expect, Jesus' followers waited in Jerusalem just as Jesus asked them to do. They continued to meet together in each other's homes to sing and pray and teach about Jesus.

Then one day, when Jesus' followers were gathered together, it happened. A sound came from heaven, a strong wind began to blow and...well, you never know what the wind will blow in!

for Overachievers

Have a four-person drama team prepare the story. Dress Peter in a Bible-time costume. Give the others bright-colored sweats and feather boas. Have a props person turn on a fan to blow on the characters at the beginning of the script. Set out three stools for the three birds.

Blow, Spirit, Blow
Based on Acts 1:4, 5, 8; 2:1–6, 14, 22–24, 37, 38, 41

Two birds enter staggering backward against the wind and flapping like crazy.

Dilbert: Whoa, Doris, what was that?

Doris: (*smoothing her feathers*) A rush of wind like I've never seen before, that's for sure!

Dilbert: No kiddin'! We doves don't usually get our feathers ruffled like that.

Doris: No, Dilbert my sweet. We're lovey doves! We just sit around on the rooftops in Jerusalem and coo sweetly to each other.

Doris and Dilbert lean toward each other and bat their eyes lovingly. Perry Pigeon enters flying backward and lands on his bottom.

Perry: Well, don't just stand there. Give me a hand—er a wing, will ya?

Dilbert: Sure, buddy. Aren't you a little out of your territory?

Perry: Whaddya mean by that?

Doris: No offense. It's just that you pigeon types usually hang around a little closer to the ground, like in the temple court.

Doris: Come perch with us. We're sheltered from the wind over here.

Perry: Don't mind if I do. *(sits on a stool)* Whew. That was some wind, wasn't it? Hey, there's a pretty nice view from here.

Dilbert: Yeah! *(points)* That's the room where Jesus' disciples always meet.

Perry: Jesus' disciples? Who is Jesus?

Doris: You must be the only bird in Jerusalem who hasn't heard of Jesus.

Perry: The family and I just flew in last week. We've spent most of our lives over by the Great Sea, actually.

Doris: Oh, so you're newcomers.

Perry: Yeah. So who's Jesus? Is he a bird?

Dilbert: Oh, no. Jesus is the Son of God. He spent a lot of time here in Jerusalem, and up by the Sea of Galilee.

Perry: Is he down in that room?

Dilbert: Nope. He's in heaven.

Perry: *(cleans out ear)* Sorry. For a minute there I thought you said he was in heaven.

Doris: The religious leaders were jealous because all the people were following Jesus, so they had him put to death. But he rose from the dead and appeared to his followers. Then, just a few weeks ago, he rose to heaven from that hill over there. *(points)*

Doris: Before he left, he told his followers that the Holy Spirit would come and help them carry on his work.

(The birds flap and try to stay on their stools as another huge rush of wind blows through.)

Perry: There's that wind again! Is it always this windy in Jerusalem?

Dilbert: Huh-uh. This is no ordinary blow.

Doris: *(points)* Look! The wind is blowing through the room where Jesus' followers are waiting!

Perry: That's not all that's happening in there. Do you see what I see?

Dilbert: You mean little flames on top of everybody's head?

Perry: Yep. And now everybody's talking—in all kinds of different languages!

Dilbert: And crowds of people are starting to gather. One of them is standing up to talk to the crowd. Isn't that the one they call Peter?

Peter enters and speaks to the audience.

Peter: What's happening here is what the prophet Joel spoke about. "I will pour my Spirit out on all people…and everyone who calls on the name of the Lord will be saved."

Peter exits.

Dilbert: The wind, the fire, people speaking in different languages…I think it's the Holy Spirit that Jesus promised.

Doris: You're right. And God's power is helping the disciples tell the crowd all about Jesus. That's amazing.

Dilbert: Since Jesus was put to death a few weeks ago, his disciples have stayed pretty much out of sight. But now they're all out in the street preaching about Jesus just as boldly as you please.

Dilbert: Look! Everyone's headed for the river. I'll bet they're going to be baptized.

Perry: Baptized?

Doris: People do that to show they believe in Jesus. It's sort of like showing that their sins are washed away.

Dilbert: Come on—we'll show you.

Doris and Dilbert circle once, then fly away. Perry watches, then starts flapping furiously to catch up.

Pretty cool! Our little flock of feathered friends got blown away by the amazing things that happened when the Holy Spirit came. Let's see if you can wing it through these questions. Toss the four numbered balls to different parts of the room.

Bring the kids with the balls to the front one-by-one and ask these questions. Allow kids to get help from the group if they need it. After each correct answer, let kids drop their balls into a bag.

 ■ **What caused the big wind at the beginning of the story?**

 ■ **Besides the wind, what other signs from God showed that Holy Spirit had come?**

 ■ **What did God's people start to do?**

 ■ **Did anyone listen to them? What did they do?**

The disciples waited in Jerusalem just as Jesus had told them. Days stretched into weeks and weeks into a month. Some of them must have begun to wonder what in the world Jesus had been talking about. But Jesus had promised that the Holy Spirit would come, so they obeyed and waited and prayed together. Then, WHOOSH! God's Spirit filled the room where they were praying and all kinds of wonderful things began to happen.

Bible Verse
You will receive power when the Holy Spirit comes on you; and you will be my witnesses.
Acts 1:8

Today in your shepherd groups, you'll get to make a fun flying reminder of how the Holy Spirit works in the hearts of those who love Jesus.

Dismiss kids to their shepherd groups.

2 Shepherd's Spot

Gather your small group and help kids find Acts 1 in their Bibles.

Today's story starts a new part of the Bible. You may remember that the first four books of the New Testament tell us about Jesus' life. Now we're in the book of Acts. It tells us the last things Jesus said on earth and how he went to heaven. Then we learn how the Holy Spirit came and helped the disciples spread the Good News about Jesus. Let's read what happened the day God sent the Holy Spirit to Jesus' disciples.

Have volunteers take turns reading Acts 1:4–8, 2:1–6 aloud.

- **Why do you think Jesus wanted his disciples to wait in Jerusalem until the Holy Spirit came?**

- **What do you think was most amazing about what happened that day?**

Pass out the "Wind of the Spirit" handout. **Lots of times you'll see a dove used as a symbol of the Holy Spirit. This is a really hard question, but someone might just know the answer.**

- **When did the Holy Spirit appear like a dove?** (*At the very beginning of Jesus' ministry, when John baptized Jesus.*)

- **Based on today's story, what other symbols could we use to represent the Holy Spirit?** (*Wind; flames.*)

God sent the Holy Spirit for a reason: to help us do his work here on earth. We don't see the Holy Spirit, but we feel his presence—just like the wind. Today we're going to make a dove that flies to remind us of how the Holy Spirit "blew in" to the room where Jesus' disciples were waiting.

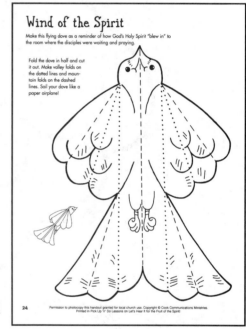

Wind of the Spirit

Make this flying dove as a reminder of how God's Holy Spirit "blew in" to the room where the disciples were waiting and praying.

Fold the dove in half and cut it out. Make valley folds on the dotted lines and mountain folds on the dashed lines. Sail your dove like a paper airplane!

24 Permission to photocopy this handout granted for local church use. Copyright © Cook Communications Ministries.
Printed in Pick Up 'n' Do Lessons on Let's Hear It for the Fruit of the Spirit!

Have kids fold the dove in half, then cut it out on the heavy line. **This folds almost like a paper airplane. Make valley folds on the dotted lines and mountain folds on the dashed lines. Then we'll slide a paper clip onto the dove's beak and see how it flies.**

Give kids time to share prayer concerns, then close in prayer. **Heavenly Father, we know how you sent your Holy Spirit to the disciples so they could tell everyone about Jesus. We want to do that kind of work too. Help us open our hearts to what the Holy Spirit has to say. Today we pray for** (mention each child's requests). **Guide us and work through us we pray. In Jesus' name, amen.**

Wind of the Spirit

Make this flying dove as a reminder of how God's Holy Spirit "blew in" to the room where the disciples were waiting and praying.

Fold the dove in half and cut it out. Make valley folds on the dotted lines and mountain folds on the dashed lines. Sail your dove like a paper airplane!

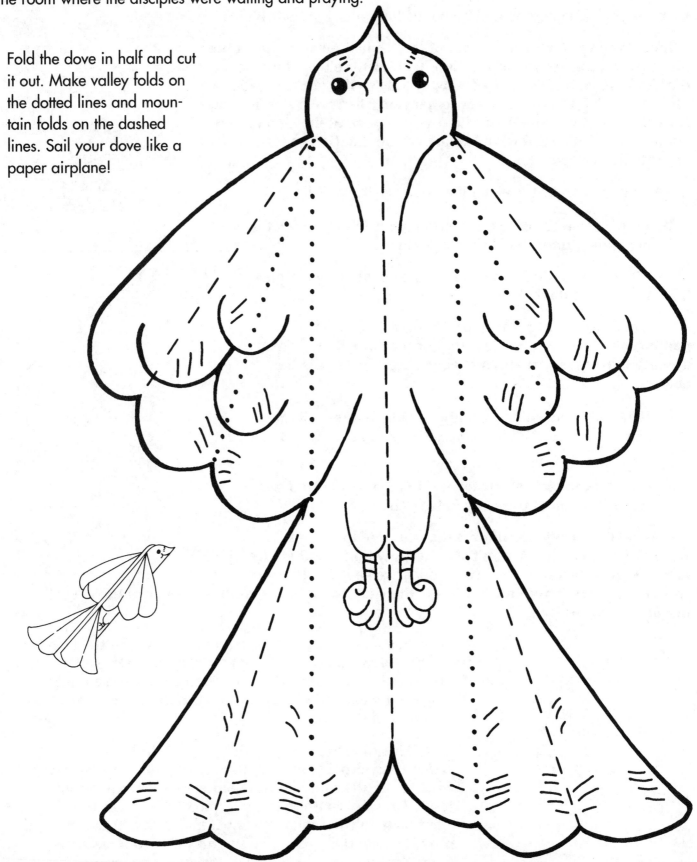

On the day of Pentecost, the people heard a sound like a mighty wind fill the house. Wind is a powerful thing—especially when it comes from heaven! The Holy Spirit helps us move along to do God's work. Let's make wind-powered racers to remind us of God's power.

Get List:
☐ lightweight balsa wood
☐ ruler
☐ cardboard
☐ patterns for 1-inch circles
☐ 8 or 10-inch balloons
☐ plastic drinking straws
☐ masking tape
☐ wood glue
☐ push pins
☐ scissors
Optional
☐ hot glue gun
☐ string

Make lightweight "cars" to illustrate the power of wind and the Holy Spirit as heard in today's story. Before class, score and snap the balsa wood into 6- and 4 -inch strips. Show kids how to glue two lengths of wood together to form a cross. You may want to have an adult helper hot glue the crosses, but be sure to have kids keep a safe distance. Have kids cut three 1-inch cardboard wheels for their cars. Encourage older kids to help younger kids cut the wheels.

Have each child take a balloon, a straw and three push pins. Hold up one of the balsa wood crosses. **When Jesus died on the cross, his disciples were alone and afraid. But Jesus loved them too much to leave them alone. With the Holy Spirit, they would have the confidence and power to tell others about his promises. Jesus promises us the same!**

Demonstrate as you work alongside your kids. **Gently pin a wheel to each end of the short piece of balsa wood.** Pause as kids' work. **Now pin the third wheel up to either side of the longer piece. Most cars have four wheels, but we don't need four wheels for our peppy little racers.**

Slide the straw inside the balloon but not all the way. You'll use the straw to blow up the balloon in just a bit! Tightly tape just the neck of the balloon (with the straw inserted) **to your wood racer. Blow up the balloon through the straw. Block the end of the straw with your thumb to keep the air in place. Put your racer on the floor. Release. Zzzzzzoooom!**

■ **How is blowing air into the balloon like the Holy Spirit working in us?**

When the Holy Spirit works in us, he gives us power to do God's work. Live in God's power!

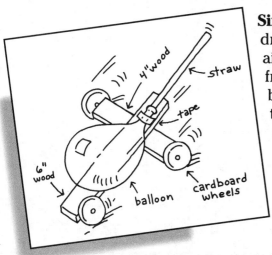

4"wood
straw
tape
6" wood
balloon
cardboard wheels

Simpler Option: Cut a 10-foot piece of string. Have two children hold the ends. Carefully tape a straw parallel to a large air-filled balloon. Pinch the end of the balloon to keep the air from escaping. Thread the string through the straw. (The balloon's nozzle should face to the side). Release! Watch as the balloon travels across the room—with a message attached, if you wish. Provide a fresh balloon and straw for each child.

Fold down the corners to start your paper airplane.

SPECIAL DELIVERY

TO

Do God's work.

☆ (A violent wind, tongues of fire appeared on the disciples, the Holy Spirit came? speaking of other languages.)

Today at church we learned that the Holy Spirit came at Pentecost. What amazing things happened when the Holy Spirit came!

Bible Verse

You will receive power when the Holy Spirit comes on you; and you will be my witnesses.

Acts 1:8

◊ How can we open ourselves so God's Holy Spirit will work in our hearts?

◊ One way our family can do God's work is:

Time for a fragrant cup of tea or hot chocolate! Get help from Mom or Dad to put on the kettle and boil some water. Watch as the heat wisps curl just above the cup's rim as you pour the water in your cup. Stir and breathe in the warm, sweet smell. Take a sip. Feel how the warmth touches your lips, tongue, throat, and finally fills your tummy! Now imagine being filled with Holy Spirit much the same way, as God prepares you to do his work.

☆ Family FUN ☆

Live It!

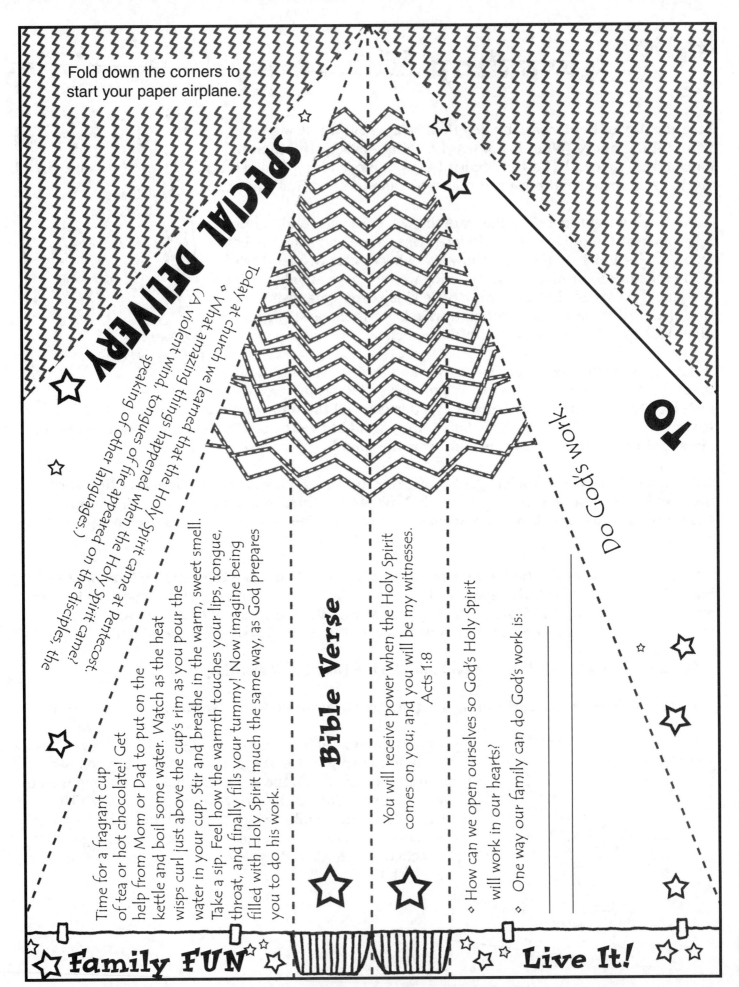

For Goodness' Sake!

Option

Get Set
LARGE GROUP ■ Greet kids and do a puppet skit. Schooner discovers that God's goodness shines through his people.

❑ large bird puppet   ❑ puppeteer

1

Bible 4U! Instant Drama
LARGE GROUP ■ A brother and sister share letters about how God's people in the early church shared with each other.

❑ 2 actors   ❑ copies of pp. 30-31, God's Goodness script   ❑ 4 numbered balls
Optional: ❑ 2 Bible-time costumes   ❑ 2 writing tables   ❑ 2 quill pens   ❑ 2 ink bottles

2

Shepherd's Spot
SMALL GROUP ■ Use the "Treasures!" handout to help kids identify what they can share.

❑ Bibles   ❑ pencils   ❑ scissors   ❑ craft knife   ❑ copies of p. 34, Treasures!
❑ copies of p. 36, Special Delivery

Option

Workshop Wonders
SMALL GROUP ■ Make a "shining" snack and talk about what it means to shine with God's goodness.

❑ paper plates   ❑ plastic knives and forks   ❑ can opener   ❑ pineapple rings
❑ bananas   ❑ salad dressing   ❑ maraschino cherries

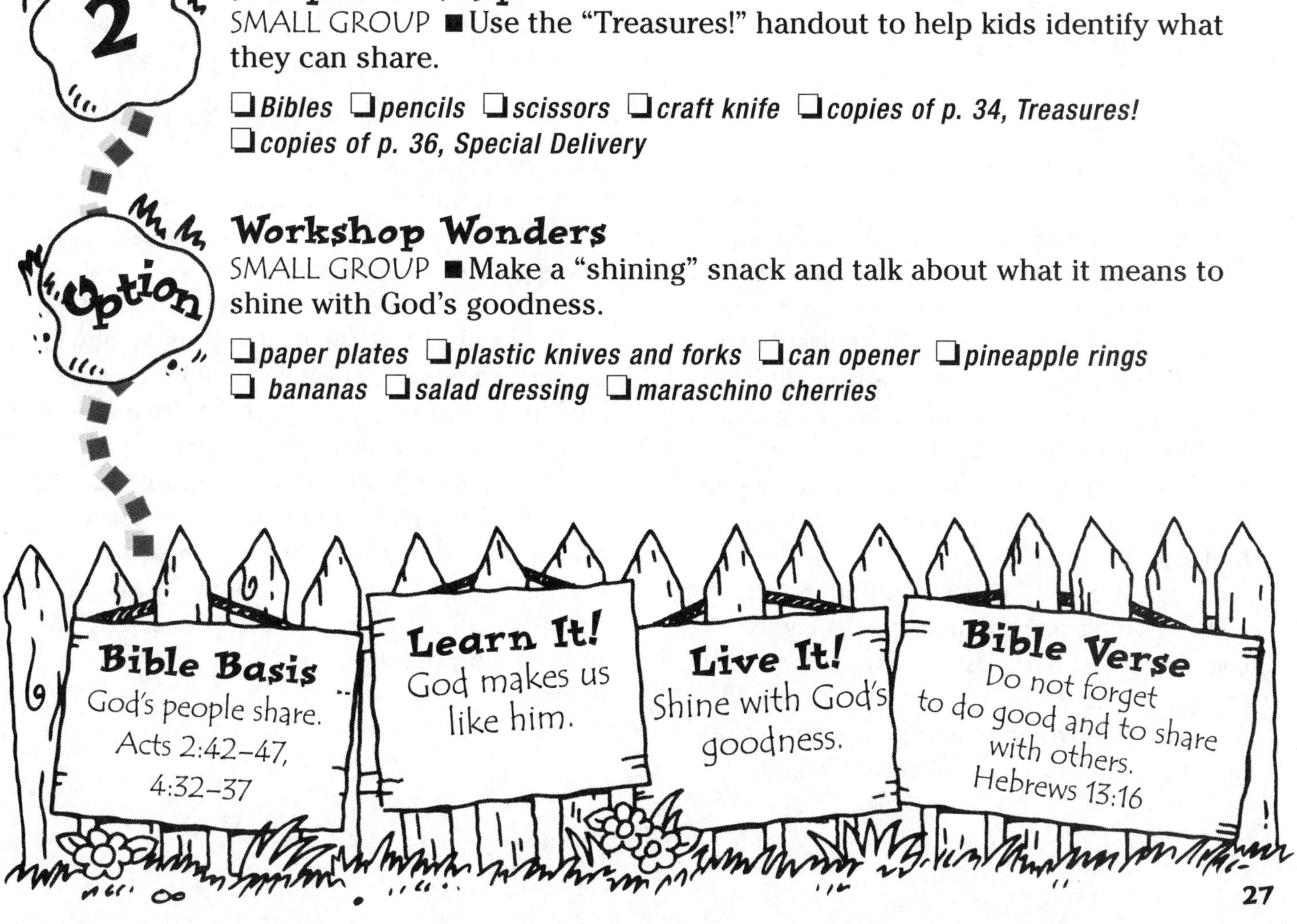

Bible Basis
God's people share.
Acts 2:42–47,
4:32–37

Learn It!
God makes us
like him.

Live It!
Shine with God's
goodness.

Bible Verse
Do not forget
to do good and to share
with others.
Hebrews 13:16

Quick Takes

Acts 2:42–47; 4:32–37

2:42 They devoted themselves to the apostles' teaching and to the fellowship, to the breaking of bread and to prayer.
43 Everyone was filled with awe, and many wonders and miraculous signs were done by the apostles.
44 All the believers were together and had everything in common.
45 Selling their possessions and goods, they gave to anyone as he had need.
46 Every day they continued to meet together in the temple courts. They broke bread in their homes and ate together with glad and sincere hearts,
47 praising God and enjoying the favor of all the people. And the Lord added to their number daily those who were being saved.
4:32 All the believers were one in heart and mind. No one claimed that any of his possessions was his own, but they shared everything they had.
33 With great power the apostles continued to testify to the resurrection of the Lord Jesus, and much grace was upon them all.
34 There were no needy persons among them. For from time to time those who owned lands or houses sold them, brought the money from the sales
35 and put it at the apostles' feet, and it was distributed to anyone as he had need.
36 Joseph, a Levite from Cyprus, whom the apostles called Barnabas (which means Son of Encouragement),
37 sold a field he owned and brought the money and put it at the apostles' feet.

Insights

From the time we come to know Christ, we experience a growing desire to reflect God's goodness. Sometimes that desire conflicts with our self-preserving nature. It's natural to want more for ourselves: it is the Holy Spirit that creates in us a desire to see first to the needs of others, even if it means significantly diminishing our own wealth. Realizing this conflict prompted a Christian lady who felt envious of friend's lovely home to say somewhat ruefully, "I wish I had that home and she had a better one!"

The Holy Spirit flows through our lives like a mountain stream rushing over a jagged rock. Over time, the irrepressible current smooths the jagged edges into a beautifully smooth, rounded river rock. This rushing of the Holy Spirit through the lives of early Christians prompted them to carefully tend to each other's needs. God's goodness expressed itself through the early church in non-material ways as well. They spent time praying and praising together. And their goodness was so evident to the community that more and more people embraced Jesus each day.

Today's lesson sets an ideal before kids. As we look at the fruit of the spirit expressed through early believers, we discover a standard that may seem unattainable. Assure kids that it's God who brings forth this wonderful fruit by working in submissive, obedient hearts.

Get Set

Open with lively music, then greet the kids. **I'm glad you're here today because there's no better place to be than with those who "share and shine" with God's goodness. And I have a friend here who would share his last piece of pineapple with us. Howdy, Schooner!** *Schooner pops up.*

Schooner: Did I hear the word pineapple?

Leader: Yes.

Schooner: Is it the dried kind or the fresh kind?

Leader: What?

Schooner: The pineapple.

Leader: No. I was just saying …

Schooner: 'Cause dried pineapple gives me hives.

Leader: What a minute. Parrots get hives…from fruit?

Schooner: Well, I can't speak for all parrots. This one does.

Leader: I…I see.

Schooner: So where is it?

Leader: Where's what, Schooner?

Schooner: The fresh pineapple swimming in sweet, clear juice?

Leader: Hold on. I was just using that as an example. There is no pineapple…THE PINEAPPLE HAS LEFT THE BUILDING!

Schooner: Bummer. Cause if we had some, I'd share my last piece with you. And with all of you! *(nods head to the group)*

Leader: That was my point all along, Schooner!

Schooner: I'm glad we think alike, boss.

Leader: The believers in today's Bible story were also "one in heart and mind." (Acts 4:32)

Schooner: *(lays his head against the Leader's heart)* Yep, we're definitely on the same beat. You'd share your last piece of pineapple with me, wouldn't you?

Leader: You know I would, buddy. In today's Bible story we're going to hear about people who shared a lot more than pineapple with each other.

Schooner: Really? They shared birdseed too?

Leader: They were just full of goodness! And goodness is a fruit of the spirit.

Schooner: Is pineapple a fruit of the spirit?

Leader: No. When the Holy Spirit works in our lives, all kinds of wonderful things come spilling out of our heart. Goodness is one of them.

Schooner: *Schweet!* I'm not sure whether I'd rather be full of goodness or full of pineapple.

Leader: The people in today's story were so full of goodness that they shared everything they had—including houses and land.

Schooner: Whoa—that's some kind of goodness. I don't know if I could ever share like that. I'm pretty fond of my nest.

Leader: It's the Holy Spirit who gives that kind of goodness. No one went hungry or needed a home. Jesus' followers took care of each other.

Schooner: So if the pineapple basket was empty and my nest blew away, they would have taken care of me.

Leader: That's how it worked.

Schooner: Those people really were good, boss.

Leader: Everyone was amazed at how they shared, and more people believed in Jesus.

Schooner: It must have been awesome to live back then.

Leader: The Holy Spirit works in our lives the same way. He makes God's goodness shine from our lives.

Schooner: You know, when I look around this room I see a lot of God's goodness.

Leader: I'm glad to hear that.

Schooner: Yeah! These kids really care for each other, don't they? And you care for them.

Leader: I do care for them. All because of what God does in my heart.

Schooner: That kind of goodness is even better than pineapple. I wanna hear more about it.

Leader: Then let's move on to Bible 4U!

1 Bible 4U!

Welcome back to Bible 4U! Theater, where the stories of the Bible jump off the pages and into our classroom. Speaking of our classroom, this is a great church, isn't it? Can some of you tell me what you like about going to church? *Pause to field a few answers.*

We're thankful to God that we can meet in this building, but this isn't how church has always been. Long ago, just after Jesus died and rose again; his followers didn't meet in church buildings like this one. Sometimes they met in the temple in Jerusalem, but they also met in homes. When they came together for church, they listened to God's Word, prayed and gave praise to God just like we do, but they also did some things differently. They often ate together, with everyone bringing food to share. And what do you think happened when some people in the church didn't have enough food? Or when they had other needs? That's what we're about to find out.

Let me introduce you to my friend Simeon. He's been writing letters to his dear sister Hannah, who lives in a nearby town.

Instant Prep
You'll need two people to play the roles of Simeon and Hannah. You may want to play one of the roles and have a student play the other. Or choose two children to read the parts. Your actors will need copies of the "God's Goodness" script below.

for Overachievers
Set up desks on opposite ends of your stage. Dress Simeon and Hannah in robes and give them rolled paper scrolls, quill pens and ink pots. Have them sit at the two desks and pretend to write as they read their parts.

God's Goodness
Based on Acts 2:42–47; 4:32–37

Simeon: *(reads aloud as he pretends to write)*
Dear Hannah,
The weather's fine here in Jerusalem. How are things up in Galilee? My goat Gertie has been grumpy lately, and she's not giving much milk. Not much else to report. Things have been fairly quiet since they crucified that prophet Jesus. After he died, we haven't heard much from his followers. It's better that way, I guess. Bye for now.
　　　　　　Your loving brother, Simeon

Hannah: *(also writing)*
Dear Simmy,
We're having lovely spring weather up here and the fishing is great. Glad things have calmed down in Jerusalem since that whole thing with Jesus is over. It's always scary when the Romans get involved. By the way, I have just the thing for a grumpy goat: a little honey in her barley. Keep me posted on how she's doing.
　　　　　　　　Love, Hannah

Simeon:
Dear Hannah,
Remember what I said about things being quiet in Jerusalem? Well, things have changed. Do you remember my neighbor Barney? People have been coming and going

at his place non-stop. Barney is one of Jesus' followers. He says Jesus rose from the dead. I wonder what that's all about! It must have something to do with the crowd at his house. I'll keep an eye on things and let you know.

Sincerely, Simeon

P.S. Gertie turned up her nose at the barley and honey. She's still grumpy and doesn't give much milk.

Hannah:

Dear Simeon,

Sorry Gertie still has the grumpies. My neighbor says to take her on a long walk to the river—that may get the kinks out of her system. Who knows? She may be upset at all the people coming and going at Barney's house. Goats like their peace and quiet. Tell me more about what's going on over there. If they get too rowdy, you could always complain to the Romans. Stay in touch.

With love, Hannah

Simeon:

Dearest Hannah,

The crowds at Barney's house get bigger every day. But they don't bother me. They're the happiest, kindest people I've ever seen. Some of them arrive with lots of food, while others arrive with no food and looking hungry. But they all leave looking as if they've eaten their fill. Some arrive with tattered clothes. Others arrive with bags of extra clothing. When they leave, the poor people are wearing the clothes that the others brought. There's some serious sharing going on there. By the way, Gertie's finally gotten used to their coming and going. She's given lots of milk and it makes the best cheese. Yum!

Your loving brother, Simeon

Hannah:

Dear Simmy,

I like the sound of what's happening at your neighbor's house. Didn't you say that Barney and his friends were followers of Jesus? I remember when Jesus taught on a hillside not far from here. When the crowd got

hungry, he fed them as much bread and fish as they wanted. Sounds like his followers are sharing like he did. Maybe you ought to offer some of that goat cheese you've been bragging about.

Hugs and Kisses, Hannah

Simeon:

Dear Hannah,

You give the best advice. I took some of my goat cheese over to Barney's house yesterday, and all I can say is, it's the best thing I've ever done. I walked in and people were praying and singing together. They told me that Jesus rose from the dead and went to heaven. And then he sent the Holy Spirit to help his followers carry on his work. Hannah, these people just shine with God's goodness. I could tell that everything they were talking about was real. I believe in Jesus and yesterday I was baptized. Later in the day Barney sold a big field that he owns down the road. Then he turned right around and gave the money to Jesus' disciples so they can use it to help God's people. I want you to meet these people for yourself.

Love, Simeon

Hannah:

Dear Simeon,

I've never heard you so excited about anything! You're right—I need to come to see what's going on there. Who would ever believe people could be so full of goodness? This can only come from God. Is there anything you want me to bring when I come?

See you soon, Hannah

Simeon:

Dear Hannah,

I can't wait for you to get here. Yes, there's something I'd like you to bring—anything you can give to help the poor. Didn't your goat have twins this year? If you can bring a goat along we can make more cheese for my friends in the church. And bring a couple of friends, too. We need all the help we can get spreading the Good News about Jesus.

Love, Simeon

Bible 4U!

Well, what do you think of that? Sounds like Jesus' followers were so full of God's goodness that more and more people joined them every day. Let's find out who's on the ball this morning. Toss out four numbered balls to different parts of the room.

Stand up if you have ball #1. Bring the kids with the balls to the front one-by-one and ask these questions. Allow kids to get help from the group if they need it. After each correct answer, let kids drop their balls into a bag.

■ Where did Jesus' followers meet after he died and rose again?

■ How were their church meetings similar to ours and how were they different?

■ How did Jesus' followers learn to share?

■ How does God's goodness show through what we do in our church?

All right! You're beginning to understand what happens when the Holy Spirit works in peoples' live they start brimming over with God's goodness. In today's story, we saw that goodness show itself in sharing. Jesus' followers really caught everyone's attention. They were so full of goodness that other people couldn't help noticing. It wasn't hard to see that Jesus made all the difference in their lives, so the church grew by leaps and bounds!

Bible Verse
Do not forget to do good and to share with others.
Hebrews 13:16

I'm sure it wasn't always easy for Jesus' followers to share everything they had. Only God's Holy Spirit can change us into such giving, caring people. But guess what—when we do that, people around us will notice that we're acting like Jesus. And just like Simeon in today's story, our neighbors might even want to follow Jesus because they see God's goodness in our lives. That's one reason Hebrews 13:16 tells us, "Do not forget to do good and to share with others." Today in your shepherd groups, you'll learn more about sharing God's goodness with the people around you.

 *Dismiss kids to their shepherd groups.*

2 Shepherd's Spot

Gather your small group and help kids find Acts 2:42–47, 4:32–37 in their Bibles.

In today's story we find out what happens when Jesus' followers form the early church and begin to do God's work. Let's read about it from the Bible. As we read, think about how the very first church compares to our church today.

Have volunteers take turns reading Acts 2:42–47, 4:32–37 aloud.

■ Do you wish you had been part of this church? Explain.

■ What made these people want to take such good care of each other?

Before God works in our hearts, it's easy to think about me-me-ME! But when we trust Jesus with our lives and the Holy Spirit begins to work in our hearts, that changes. The Holy Spirit helps us see the needs of others, and we begin to think of ways we can meet their needs. Before we know it, God's goodness shines through our lives, just as it did in the lives of the early Christians.

It's easy to think, "I don't have much to share. I'm not rich and I'm just a kid." Well, guess what. Letting God's goodness spill out of your life doesn't have anything to do with how much money you have or how old you are.

■ What are some good things from God you can share that you can't touch or feel? *(Words of encouragement; the Good News about Jesus; promises to pray for someone.)*

Pass out the "Treasures!" handouts. **God works through each of us in different ways. Think for a moment about the treasure of God's goodness you can share with others. Write your treasures to share on the Treasure Cards. Then cut and fold the box and slip the** **Treasure Cards inside.** Help kids cut out the cards and box on the heavy lines. Open the slit in the box with a craft knife, then fold the box together and close it by slipping the tab into the slit.

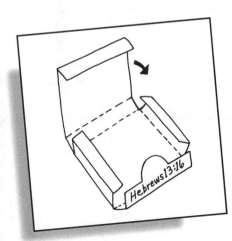

Let's think about people who need God's goodness in their lives. When I pause in my prayer, add the names of people you're thinking of. **Dear Lord, we want to shine with your goodness. We pray that you'll open our hearts to people whose lives you can touch through us. We think especially of** (let kids name people). **Please allow your Holy Spirit to work in our hearts so your goodness shines through us. In Jesus' name, amen.**

Treasures!

When we allow the Holy Spirit to work in our lives, God's goodness spills over onto everyone around us. What treasures from God do you have to share? A word of encouragement, help with a hard task, a promise to pray for someone? Fill your treasure box with God's goodness, then give it away!

Hebrews 13:16

Treasures to Share

Treasure Card

Treasure Card

Do not forget to do good and to share with others.

Gather kids around a table. Have them help you set out the supplies and open and drain the canned pineapple rings.

Get List:
- plastic tablecloth
- paper plates
- plastic knives and forks
- can opener
- canned pineapple rings
- bananas
- salad dressing
- maraschino cherries

Today we learned about the lives of people in the early church. They did things a little differently than we do today!

■ **How did the people of the early church live?**

■ **Why do you think the church kept growing every day?**

The Bible tells us that everyone was "filled with awe" when they saw what was going on in the early church. Jesus' apostles did miracles, God's people shared everything they had and took care of each other, and they were always filled with joy and praising God. God's goodness shone so brightly that more people believed in Jesus every day!

Goodness is the first fruit of the spirit that we're learning about. Let's celebrate with a fruity treat that will remind us what happens when we allow God's goodness to shine from our lives.

Have kids work in trios to assemble their treats. **You and your partners will share one banana. You'll each need one of everything else.** Show kids how to build a candle salad. Place a pineapple ring on a plate. Peel and cut a banana in three pieces. Put a dab of salad dressing inside the pineapple ring then place the banana in it upright to form a candle. Add another dab of salad dressing to the tip of the banana and stick on a cherry to represent the flame.

Voilà—a glowing fruity treat! Let's enjoy.

■ **What do you think it means to shine with God's goodness?**

We had a simple recipe for our treat, but there's no simple recipe for goodness. We don't wake up one morning and decide, "I'm just going to be full of God's goodness today." Goodness comes from a life that's open to the Holy Spirit—it's something God creates in our hearts.

I hope you'll make this fruity treat for your family this week. Tell about the people in the early church. As you give thanks for your treat, open your hearts to God and pray together that God would fill you with his goodness!

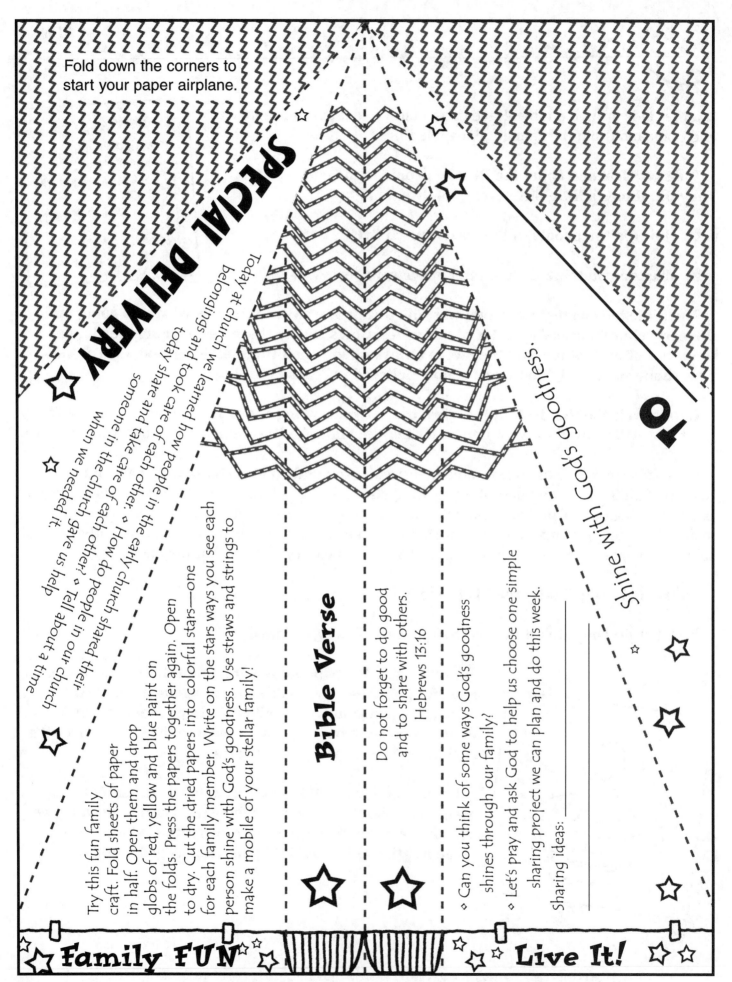

Fold down the corners to start your paper airplane.

SPECIAL DELIVERY

TO

Shine with God's goodness.

Today at church we learned how people in the early church shared their belongings and took care of each other. ◇ How do people in our church today share and take care of each other? ◇ Tell about a time someone in the church gave us help when we needed it.

Bible Verse

Do not forget to do good and to share with others.
Hebrews 13:16

◇ Can you think of some ways God's goodness shines through our family?

◇ Let's pray and ask God to help us choose one simple sharing project we can plan and do this week.

Sharing ideas: _____

Try this fun family craft. Fold sheets of paper in half. Open them and drop globs of red, yellow and blue paint on the folds. Press the papers together again. Open to dry. Cut the dried papers into colorful stars—one for each family member. Write on the stars ways you see each person shine with God's goodness. Use straws and strings to make a mobile of your stellar family!

☆ Family FUN ☆   ☆ Live It! ☆

Jump, Shout, Knock Yourself Out!

Option

Get Set
LARGE GROUP ■ Greet kids and do a puppet skit. Schooner tries to guess the word that makes all the difference in today's Bible story.

❏ *large bird puppet* ❏ *puppeteer*

1

Bible 4U! Instant Drama
LARGE GROUP ■ Two strong legs and a thankful heart help a beggar share his miraculous story.

❏ *1 actor* ❏ *copies of pp. 40-41, One Giant Leap script* ❏ *4 numbered balls*
Optional: ❏ *temple gate setting* ❏ *Bibletime costumes*

2

Shepherd's Spot
SMALL GROUP ■ Use the "A New View" handout to help kids plan how to reach out to others in love.

❏ *Bibles* ❏ *pencils* ❏ *scissors* ❏ *copies of p. 44, A New View handout*
❏ *copies of p. 46, Special Delivery*

Option

Workshop Wonders
SMALL GROUP ■ Bring a sweet and loving touch to people in your church with this "handy" and colorful craft.

❏ *disposable latex gloves* ❏ *black permanent markers* ❏ *colored art tissue*
❏ *wrapped candy* ❏ *gift ribbon* Optional: ❏ *foil heart stickers* ❏ *loose candy*

Bible Basis
Peter heals a beggar at the Temple.
Acts 3:1–16

Learn It!
Our loving touch brings people to God.

Live It!
Be loving.

Bible Verse
The fruit of the Spirit is love, joy, peace, patience, kindness, goodness, faithfulness, gentleness and self control.
Galatians 5:22, 23

3:1 One day Peter and John were going up to the temple at the time of prayer—at three in the afternoon.

2 Now a man crippled from birth was being carried to the temple gate called Beautiful, where he was put every day to beg from those going into the temple courts.

3 When he saw Peter and John about to enter, he asked them for money.

4 Peter looked straight at him, as did John. Then Peter said, "Look at us!"

5 So the man gave them his attention, expecting to get something from them.

6 Then Peter said, "Silver or gold I do not have, but what I have I give you. In the name of Jesus Christ of Nazareth, walk."

7 Taking him by the right hand, he helped him up, and instantly the man's feet and ankles became strong.

8 He jumped to his feet and began to walk. Then he went with them into the temple courts, walking and jumping, and praising God.

9 When all the people saw him walking and praising God,

10 they recognized him as the same man who used to sit begging at the temple gate called Beautiful, and they were filled with wonder and amazement at what had happened to him.

11 While the beggar held on to Peter and John, all the people were astonished and came running to them in the place called Solomon's Colonnade.

12 When Peter saw this, he said to them: "Men of Israel, why does this surprise you? Why do you stare at us as if by our own power or godliness we had made this man walk?

13 The God of Abraham, Isaac and Jacob, the God of our fathers, has glorified his servant Jesus. You handed him over to be killed, and you disowned him before Pilate, though he had decided to let him go.

14 You disowned the Holy and Righteous One and asked that a murderer be released to you.

15 You killed the author of life, but God raised him from the dead. We are witnesses of this.

16 By faith in the name of Jesus, this man whom you see and know was made strong. It is Jesus' name and the faith that comes through him that has given this complete healing to him, as you can all see."

Insights

While beggars are not a common sight in our society, things were different in Bible times. If a disabled person had no family to rely on, begging was the expected way to eke out an existence. Giving to the poor was encouraged over and over in the Law: "There will always be poor people in the land. Therefore I command you to be openhanded toward your brothers and toward the poor and needy in your land" (Deuteronomy 15:11).

The beggar at the temple gate placed himself wisely. Worshipers going up for prayer would be mindful of God's laws. If there was ever a place where people would be in an unusually compassionate frame of mind, this was it. So when Peter "looked straight at him," the beggar had good reason to be hopeful. But nothing could have prepared him for the gift he was about to receive.

This is a "goose bumps" passage! Peter's intense look, the disabled man's anticipation, then the bold proclamation, "In the name of Jesus Christ of Nazareth, walk." Peter's strong fisherman's hands pulled the man up into a new life, strong and whole.

As Christians, we have something out of the ordinary to give. The Holy Spirit enables us to see past the superficial to the heart of people's needs. The touch of God's love we offer is nothing short of life-changing. Use this lesson to help kids see that they can touch people's lives with God's transforming love.

Open with lively music, then greet the kids. **We've gathered to talk about a very important subject. And it's something that we just can't live without. I'll give you a clue! It has four letters. Schooner, do you have any ideas?** *Schooner pops up.*

Schooner: It has four letters and makes us feel good?

Leader: Yep, and life is very sad without it.

Schooner: You know, boss, I'm a pretty smart parrot. I think I'll be able to figure this out.

Leader: While we're on the subject, what grade are you in, Schooner?

Schooner: I'm at the top perch in Parrot School.

Leader: Wonderful.

Schooner: But the sky's the limit when you're smart like me.

Leader: I see.

Schooner: Now give me a minute to think. Small word with four letters…

Leader: *(hums a tune while waiting)*

Schooner: I know! Seed.

Leader: Seed?

Schooner: Life is very sad when I don't have seeds.

Leader: Good try, but no banana.

Schooner: Ooh—I could use a nice banana right now.

Leader: Keep your focus, Schooner.

Schooner: Hey, you're the one who brought up bananas! Okay, is it something you eat?

Leader: No.

Schooner: But you really need it and life is sad without it?

Leader: Yep.

Schooner: Hmm. Can you touch it or feel it?

Leader: Not exactly.

Schooner: I'm feeling kind of stumped here.

Leader: *(chuckles)* Behold. A stumped parrot.

Schooner: Are you making fun of me?

Leader: Sorry, Schooner. It's just that you usually have all the answers. At least you think you do.

Schooner: That's getting a little personal.

Leader: *(shakes head)* Sorry. Another clue might help you. The word I'm thinking of is a fruit of the Holy Spirit.

Schooner: *(brightens)* Like the word goodness?

Leader: *(brightens also)* You remembered, Schooner! Very good.

Schooner: What about the word Jesus?

Leader: Great guess, Schooner. Jesus and this word go together perfectly. In fact, you can't have one without the other. But the word Jesus has five letters.

Schooner: *Squawk!* I give up. Tell me, boss.

Leader: The word is love, Schooner. L-O-V-E.

Schooner: Jesus and love. I should have guessed it! That was easy.

Leader: In today's Bible story, Peter, a disciple of Jesus, meets a man whose legs do not work.

Schooner: What does that have to do with love?

Leader: I'm getting to that. The man hadn't been able to walk his whole life. He relied on friends to carry him where he needed to go, mostly to beg for money.

Schooner: *(hangs head)* I feel sorry for the man.

Leader: So did Peter and his friend John.

Schooner: So did they give him money?

Leader: No.

Schooner: Oh.

Leader: But through the power of the Holy Spirit, Peter's loving touch made amazing things happen.

Schooner: I love it when that happens! So what exactly happened?

Leader: We wouldn't want to give away too much of the story.

Schooner: Let me guess. You're thinking of two words that have six letters and the number four.

Leader: You're catching on, Schooner.

Schooner: And the words are…

Leader: Bible 4U! up next.

Schooner: *(nods to the group)* Told ya! Stay tuned!

Welcome to Bible 4U! Let's join the crowd going up to the temple to pray. That's what Jewish people did every afternoon at three o'clock, the time of the daily sacrifice. Everyone stopped what they were doing and went to pray. People looked forward to going up to the temple. It was a beautiful place of worship with spacious courts and lofty columns that reminded everyone of God's glory.

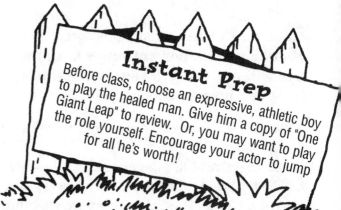

Instant Prep

Before class, choose an expressive, athletic boy to play the healed man. Give him a copy of "One Giant Leap" to review. Or, you may want to play the role yourself. Encourage your actor to jump for all he's worth!

Before Jesus died and rose again and went to heaven, he spent a lot of time at the temple. He spoke with the priests and taught the people there.

for Overachievers

Have your drama team prepare a backdrop of a street leading up to the gate of the temple with the temple shining in the background. Dress "extras" in Bible time costumes. Place some of them as beggars and others as amazed bystanders as the healed man tells the story.

Today Jesus' disciples Peter and John are on their way to the temple to pray. Wherever Peter goes there's always a lot of excitement. Peter and John were two of Jesus' closest friends, and now they're leaders of the church. They're so filled with God's spirit that it's wonderful to be around them. Let's follow them. You never know what might happen.

One Giant Leap
Acts 3:1–16

Look at me! Just look at me! I'm standing here on two strong legs; just as straight and tall as you please *(shake one leg, then the other)*. My toes wiggle—all ten of them *(wiggle toes)*. I can hop on this foot *(hop)*, and on this one *(hop on the other foot)*. Isn't that just amazing? *(jump and click heels together)*

You're not very impressed, are you? I mean, most people can stand and wiggle their toes and hop. And some can even click their heels together. But when I woke up this morning I couldn't do any of

those things. I've never been able to, all my life. When other kids were chasing sheep and goats I lay on a pallet outside the door of my house. I could do a few things to help my parents, but mostly I just sat and watched life go by.

I felt sorry for myself back then, but I had no idea how much worse life could be. After my parents died, there was no one to take care of me. No aunts, uncles or cousins. I was on my own, and I couldn't find enough work to make a living. The best thing I could do was get some friends to carry me up to the temple every day.

You see, good Jewish people go to the temple to pray and offer sacrifices every afternoon at three o'clock. So the temple was the perfect place for me to sit and beg. People who were coming to pray were thinking about God and about the Law. And the Law said to be kind to the poor and take care of them. So I sat by the temple gate day after day, hoping people would give me enough money to buy food. And I had no hope that my life would ever be any different than that…until today!

"Yes! Yes! Yes! *(jump and shout)* Praise be to the living God!"

A lot of people walked by without even looking at me today. I was getting a little worried. But then two men walked up. One was strong and burly and the other quiet and thoughtful. The big burly man looked me right in the eye. That's always a good sign. If people aren't going to give you anything, they usually look away. So I said, "Alms? Can you spare a few coins?"

The big man said, "Silver and gold I do not have, but what I have I give you. In the name of Jesus Christ of Nazareth, walk." Before I even had time to be amazed, he reached out for my hand and pulled me up. My head spun for a moment, but my legs— these legs that have never carried me one step in my whole life—stood strong. My mouth dropped open, but the men, Peter and John, just smiled at me. They walked with me into the temple court and explained

that they were followers of Jesus. They told me how he died and rose again, and that it was his power that had healed me.

Then I took one giant leap. Then another, and another! *(run around the room jumping and saying, "Praise God!")* I couldn't stop myself. These wobbly, useless legs carried me all around the temple courts. People looked at me in amazement, not just because of the noise I was making but because they recognized me as the beggar who couldn't walk. That caused a lot of people to ask questions. So, of course, Peter began to tell them about Jesus.

Look down at your legs. Stick them out straight and cross your ankles. Now touch toes with three people sitting near you. Do you know how amazing it is to do that for the very first time?

Peter and John didn't have to notice me. There are beggars all over Jerusalem. But they did. I could see God's love in their eyes. I felt his power in their touch. And that touch changed my life forever. Now I'm going to use these two good legs to walk all over this city and tell people what the love of Jesus can do. Why don't you use your legs to do the same thing!

(Exit with a little dance step)

It took just a moment to change a man's life forever. In the middle of a crowd, one man caught Peter and John's attention. When they responded with God's love, the man they healed went leaping for joy. Let's see if you can leap on the answers to questions about the story.

Toss four numbered balls to different areas of the room. Invite the kids who pick them up to come up front one-by-one and answer a question. Allow kids to get help from the group if they need it. After each correct answer, have kids drop their balls into a bag.

 ■ Why did the beggar sit where he did?

 ■ How did what Peter and John gave the beggar compare to what he was hoping to get?

 ■ Why do you think Peter and John noticed that particular beggar?

 ■ What do you think it felt like when Peter touched the beggar to pull him to his feet?

Most of the people who walked by that day just saw another beggar. He probably didn't look or smell very good. But the Holy Spirit caused Peter and John to take notice of this man. They saw a man who needed the touch of God's love.

Bible Verse
The fruit of the Spirit is love, joy, peace, patience, kindness, goodness, faithfulness, gentleness and self control.
Galatians 5:22, 23

One of the most important things the Holy Spirit gives us is a new set of eyes. With God's love, we don't see people the same way we used to. God begins to show us people's deepest needs. And he also shows us how to touch that person with his love. Our touch may not be as miraculous as Peter and John's. But you might be surprised at what a difference you can make in someone's life when you ask God to help.

When God's Holy Spirit works in our hearts we begin to think more about others and a little less about ourselves. Then we don't think, "Oh, no—there's that annoying person again!" We think, "Wow—that person is really hurting. Lord, please help me know what to do to touch that person with your love."

Today in your shepherd groups you'll discover how your loving touch can help bring people to God.

Dismiss kids to their shepherd groups.

② Shepherd's Spot

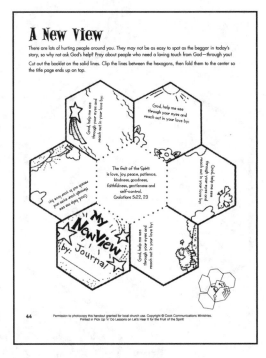

Gather your small group and help kids find Acts 3 in their Bibles.

We're getting into a really exciting part of the book of Acts. On the day of Pentecost the Holy Spirit filled the disciples with God's power. Now they're on the move in and around Jerusalem, and we're going to see some wonderful things happen!

Have volunteers take turns reading Acts 3:1–16 aloud. **The beggar was hoping for something from Peter and John, but he sure got a lot more than he expected!**

■ **What would you have thought if you passed a beggar?**

■ **Has anyone ever noticed you and given help when you needed it? Tell about it.**

The Holy Spirit helps us see people the way God sees them. Peter and John didn't see a bothersome beggar— they saw a man whose life could be completely changed by God's love and power. There are people like that around us, too. We pass them every day. But, with the help of the Holy Spirit, we can touch them with God's love. Pass out the "A New View" handout. Ask a volunteer to read Galatians 5:22, 23 aloud.

We'll run across this verse several times in the next few weeks. It tells us about the fruit God's Holy Spirit brings from our lives when we're open and obedient to him. Let's make this cool little journal and ask God to show us people who need his loving touch.

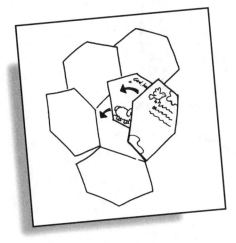

Show kids how to cut out and fold the hexagonal journal. Encourage them to take some quiet time to pray and jot down names and ideas in their journals.

Invite kids to share prayer concerns, then close with prayer. **Heavenly Father, we want to be more like you. We invite your Holy Spirit to work in our lives to bring forth the fruit of love, joy, peace, patience, kindness, goodness, faithfulness, gentleness and self-control. Help us see people through your eyes. This week we pray especially for (name kids' concerns). We ask these things in Jesus' name, amen.**

A New View

There are lots of hurting people around you. They may not be as easy to spot as the beggar in today's story, so why not ask God's help? Pray about people who need a loving touch from God—through you!

Cut out the booklet on the solid lines. Clip the lines between the hexagons, then fold them to the center so the title page ends up on top.

God, help me see through your eyes and reach out in your love by:

God, help me see through your eyes and reach out in your love by:

God, help me see through your eyes and reach out in your love by:

The fruit of the Spirit is love, joy, peace, patience, kindness, goodness, faithfulness, gentleness and self-control.
Galatians 5:22, 23

God, help me see through your eyes and reach out in your love by:

My New View Journal by: _____

God, help me see through your eyes and reach out in your love by:

To help your students along, bring a sample of this craft to class. **In today's story, Peter gave what he could to the poor beggar who couldn't walk. He didn't have gold or silver, which is what the man expected—and probably really, really wanted! Instead, Peter had compassion and love for the man. Can you imagine the man's surprise when he received healing from Peter's loving touch?**

■ **Have you ever asked God for something you really wanted, but God surprised you by giving you something better? Share your experience with the class.**

Today we're going to have fun giving a "g-loving touch" to someone who needs a touch of God's love. We'll lend a "hand" filled with surprises to someone at church today. And it will be a very sweet surprise! Hold up the glove craft you made before class for kids to see.

■ **Have you ever felt God's love through someone else's actions? Explain.**

Distribute gloves. Set out the markers and colorful tissue paper. **On the palm of your glove use your marker to draw a heart. Under the heart, print the words "The fruit of the Spirit."** Pause as kids work. **Now, on the front and back of each finger, print a fruit of the spirit. Don't remember the fruit? No need to fear Galatians 5:22, 23 is here! It just happens to be our Bible verse for today. Let's say Galatians 5:22, 23 together.**

The fruit of the Spirit is love, joy, peace, patience, kindness,
goodness, faithfulness, gentleness and self-control. Galatians 5:22, 23

Work alongside your kids as they complete the craft. **Stuff crushed pieces of tissue paper into each finger of your glove. Use different colors, if you wish.** Spread the candy treats on the table. Let's kids sample as they fill the palm of their gloves with treats. **Finish up with a bit more crushed tissue paper to hold the candy in place. Then tie off the glove with a ribbon.** Distribute the foil heart stickers and have kids stick them to their gloves. Discuss possible recipients of your handy treats, then send kids on their loving mission.

Simpler Option: Eliminate the tissue paper and fill the latex gloves with loose, rounded candy pieces or jelly beans. Mix and match candies for a colorful design. Knot closed.

Get List:
- ❑ disposable latex gloves (found at grocery and home improvement stores)
- ❑ black permanent markers
- ❑ colored art tissue
- ❑ wrapped candy
- ❑ gift ribbon

Optional
- ❑ foil heart stickers
- ❑ loose candy pieces

Printed in Pick Up 'n' Do Lessons on Let's Hear It for the Fruit of the Spirit!

45

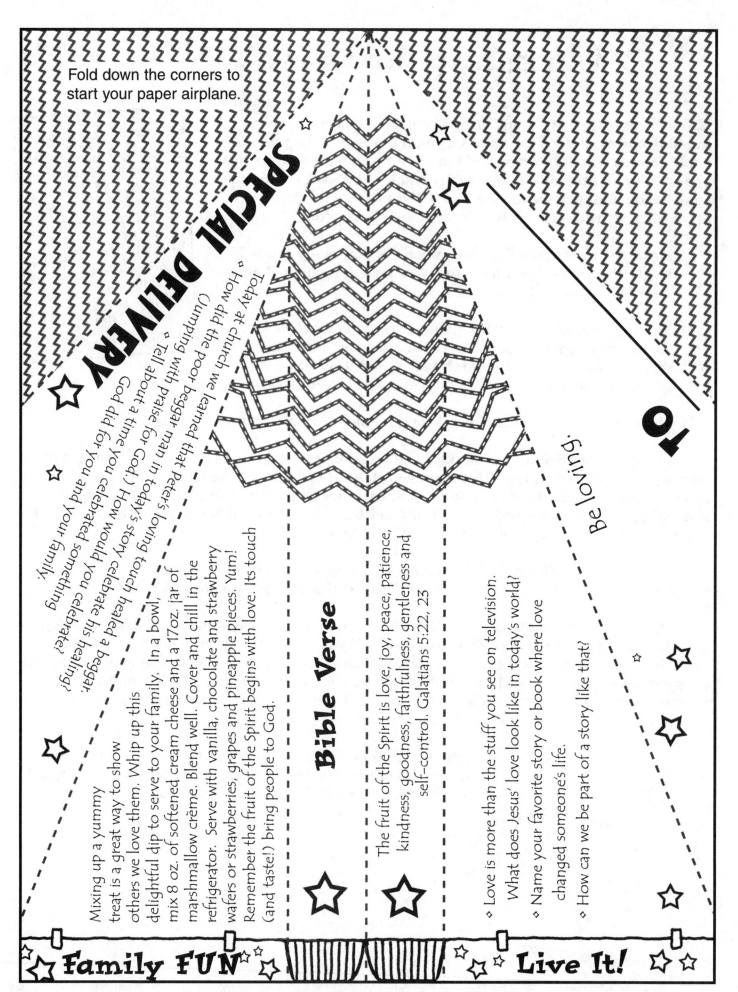

Fold down the corners to start your paper airplane.

SPECIAL DELIVERY

TO

Be loving.

Today at church we learned that Peter's loving touch healed a beggar. (Jumping with praise for God.) How did the poor beggar man in today's story touch God? Tell about a time you celebrated something God did for you and your family. How would you celebrate his healing?

Mixing up a yummy treat is a great way to show others we love them. Whip up this delightful dip to serve to your family. In a bowl, mix 8 oz. of softened cream cheese and a 17 oz. jar of marshmallow crème. Blend well. Cover and chill in the refrigerator. Serve with vanilla, chocolate and strawberry wafers or strawberries, grapes and pineapple pieces. Yum! Remember the fruit of the Spirit begins with love. Its touch (and taste!) bring people to God.

Bible Verse

The fruit of the Spirit is love, joy, peace, patience, kindness, goodness, faithfulness, gentleness and self-control. Galatians 5:22, 23

◇ Love is more than the stuff you see on television. What does Jesus' love look like in today's world?
◇ Name your favorite story or book where love changed someone's life.
◇ How can we be part of a story like that?

Family FUN

Live It!

Courage Under Fire

Get Set
Option

LARGE GROUP ■ Greet kids and do a puppet skit. Schooner learns how the Holy Spirit filled Peter and John with courage.

❏ *large bird puppet*   ❏ *puppeteer*

Bible 4U! Instant Drama
1

LARGE GROUP ■ Peter, John and the powerful high priest Annas have a vocal showdown in the city of Jerusalem. See who comes out on top!

❏ *4 actors*   ❏ *copies of pp. 50-51, Face Off script*   ❏ *4 numbered balls*
Optional: ❏ *Bibletime costumes*

Shepherd's Spot
2

SMALL GROUP ■ Pocket the change! Use this nifty handout to reassure kids that God's Spirit will help them change into confident speakers for Jesus.

❏ *Bibles*   ❏ *pencils*   ❏ *scissors*   ❏ *copies of p. 54, Pocketful of Courage handout*
❏ *copies of p. 56, Special Delivery*

Workshop Wonders
Option

SMALL GROUP ■ Make "cone-head" buddies that are ready to speak out for Jesus.

❏ *ice cream cake cones*   ❏ *cake mix*   ❏ *eggs*   ❏ *oil*   ❏ *water*   ❏ *canned frosting*
❏ *fruit-flavored cereal loops*   ❏ *oven*   *Optional:* ❏ *colored coconut*   ❏ *licorice ropes*
❏ *chow mein noodles*   ❏ *fruit leather*   ❏ *snowball snack cakes*

Bible Basis
Peter and John witness before the Sanhedrin.
Acts 4:1–13

Learn It!
The Holy Spirit gives us courage.

Live It!
Speak out for Jesus.

Bible Verse
But Peter and John replied, "We cannot help speaking about what we have seen and heard." Acts 4:20

Quick Takes

Acts 4:1–13

4:1 The priests and the captain of the temple guard and the Sadducees came up to Peter and John while they were speaking to the people.

2 They were greatly disturbed because the apostles were teaching the people and proclaiming in Jesus the resurrection of the dead.

3 They seized Peter and John, and because it was evening, they put them in jail until the next day.

4 But many who heard the message believed, and the number of men grew to about five thousand.

5 The next day the rulers, elders and teachers of the law met in Jerusalem.

6 Annas the high priest was there, and so were Caiaphas, John, Alexander and the other men of the high priest's family.

7 They had Peter and John brought before them and began to question them: "By what power or what name did you do this?"

8 Then Peter, filled with the Holy Spirit, said to them: "Rulers and elders of the people!

9 If we are being called to account today for an act of kindness shown to a cripple and are asked how he was healed,

10 then know this, you and all the people of Israel: It is by the name of Jesus Christ of Nazareth, whom you crucified but whom God raised from the dead, that this man stands before you healed.

11 He is 'the stone you builders rejected, which has become the capstone'

12 Salvation is found in no one else, for there is no other name under heaven given to men by which we must be saved."

13 When they saw the courage of Peter and John and realized that they were unschooled, ordinary men, they were astonished and they took note that these men had been with Jesus.

Insights

Rabbis and teachers of the law were the intellectual elite of Jewish society. Unlike ordinary men, they seldom worked at a trade. They memorized the books of the Law, the prophets, history and the writings (what we call wisdom literature), and they dedicated all their years of study and intellectual prowess to interpreting the scripture. In the rabbinic tradition, they knew how to argue! They would answer questions by asking another question, armed with their tremendous knowledge.

These leaders convened in the Sanhedrin, the ruling body of the Jews. They were the group who condemned Jesus. Into their intimidating presence came Peter and John, rough fishermen from the back country of Galilee. Filled with the Holy Spirit, these two disciples who had spent three years with Jesus stood with unflinching courage and proclaimed that the miraculous healing of the beggar had been done through the power of the resurrected Jesus. Their outspoken courage amazed the teachers of law.

Today's kids face intellectuals in authority who will belittle their faith in the light of what they see as "enlightened" post-modern views. Use this lesson to teach them that the Holy Spirit will give them the courage to speak God's truth in any situation they may face.

Open with lively music, then greet the kids. **Today's Bible story speaks of being filled with the Holy Spirit. The Holy Spirit gives us the courage to share Jesus with others. I'll bet our feathered friend can give us some tips on this subject. Schooner, are you there?** *Schooner pops up.*

Schooner: I've been thinking, boss.
Leader: That's a good sign!
Schooner: About what you said about being filled with the Holy Spirit.
Leader: Okay.
Schooner: So let's say it's a hot summer day.
Leader: Yes…
Schooner: And suddenly you're very thirsty.
Leader: *(nods head slowly)* I see where you're going Schooner. So you reach for a tall glass.
Schooner: No, boss. *You* reach for a glass. I don't have hands, remember?
Leader: Quite right. *I* grab a tall glass.
Schooner: And you fill it up with frosty cold lemonade.
Leader: Go on, Schooner.
Schooner: And…that's as far as I got, boss. I'm thunked out.
Leader: But you're on to something, Schooner.
Schooner: I am?
Leader: You're on somebody's arm, actually.
Schooner: That's a low blow, boss.
Leader: Back to the lemonade. I drink it up and feel refreshed.
Schooner: And you're ready to go!
Leader: In today's story the Apostle Peter was filled with the Holy Spirit. He was ready to go too.
Schooner: Go do what, boss?
Leader: Go speak to a crowd of very important people who also happened to be pretty mean.
Schooner: How mean were they?
Leader: They were the people who decided to put Jesus to death.
Schooner: *(gasps)* Peter must have been scared out of his wits! I bet he couldn't think of a single thing to say.

Leader: There's one very important thing to remember here, Schooner.
Schooner: What's that?
Leader: Peter was filled with the Holy Spirit. He stood up as bold as you please and told them that Jesus Christ is the Son of God, the salvation of the world!
Schooner: Whoa—how could he be that brave?
Leader: Think hard, Schooner.
Schooner: Well, it probably wasn't from drinking lemonade.
Leader: Keep thinking.
Schooner: Well, you said he was filled with the Holy Spirit!
Leader: Bingo!
Schooner: So the Holy Spirit gave him courage?
Leader: Right you are. And he'll do the same thing for us today.
Schooner: You mean he helps people talk about Jesus?
Leader: That's exactly right.
Schooner: What if you're kind of shy? What if you think that other people are a lot smarter? What if…
Leader: Schooner, we're talking about the Spirit of God.
Schooner: Right! And God can help us do anything.
Leader: Yep. Even talk to a roomful of mean people about Jesus.
Schooner: We need to know more about this, boss.
Leader: I couldn't agree more. That's why…
Schooner: Bible 4U! is up next!

1 Bible 4U!

Welcome to another exciting presentation of Bible 4U! Today we're going to Jerusalem where the church was just getting started. You may remember, Jerusalem was the place where Jesus was put on trial. There were many important people who didn't like Christians. In fact, the same people who put Jesus to death wanted to stop his disciples from telling everyone that he had risen from the dead.

Instant Prep

Before class, ask four volunteers to play the roles of Annas, Peter, John and the Healed Man. Give them copies of the "Face Off" script to review.

Do you remember the story of Peter and John healing the beggar who couldn't walk? That miracle caused a lot of excitement. Huge crowds of people listened to Peter preach about Jesus. The Jewish leaders saw that more and more people believed in Jesus, so they threw Peter and John into jail.

for Overachievers

Have a four-person drama team prepare the story. Dress the two apostles and the Healed Man in simple Bible time robes and sandals. Dress Annas in a dark, elegant robe. Have others from your drama team dress as priests, sit behind Annas and respond to the drama as it unfolds.

The next day Peter and John were brought into court before the very same people who condemned Jesus to death. Annas, the high priest, was in charge.

Let's step into the courtroom as Annas and Peter face off.

Face Off
Acts 4:1–13

Annas and Peter stand facing the audience. John stands in the background.

Annas: *(proudly)* My name is Annas.

Peter: *(humbly)* My name is Peter.

Annas: I am a high priest in the temple of God.

Peter: I am a follower of Jesus Christ, son of the living God.

Annas: I spend my days in the temple, teaching about the Law and the Scriptures.

Peter: I spend my days traveling, preaching and teaching people about Jesus' death and resurrection. Sometimes God uses me to heal people, like the beggar who used to sit at the temple gate.

Annas: I am highly educated. I hold the highest office in Israel.

Peter: I'm a fisherman by trade. I hardly went to school. But for three years I traveled with Jesus. My rabbi is the Son of God!

Annas: When it comes to teaching about God, this court has the final say. We got rid of Jesus and we'll get rid of his followers, too.

Peter: God is with us, and the church keeps growing. We're spreading the Good News about Jesus everywhere we go. More and more people believe in Jesus every day.

Annas: I am responsible for leading the rulers, elders and teachers of the law.

Peter: The church here in Jerusalem looks to me for leadership. The Sanhedrin may arrest me and throw me in jail, but nothing can stop me from preaching about Jesus.

Annas: Jesus' disciples are spreading the word that Jesus rose from the dead. Just yesterday Peter healed a beggar by the temple gate. So we threw Peter in jail, along with his friend John. He's probably scared that we'll do the same thing to him that we did to Jesus. I can't wait to see him shaking in his boots when he faces the Sanhedrin.

Peter: *(turns to John)* It's time to stand before the Sanhedrin and tell the truth about Jesus.

John: *(puts his hand on Peter's arm)* God will be with us.

Annas: *(to Peter and John, sternly)* By what power or name did you heal that man?

(Healed Man comes forward and faces Annas with arms crossed.)

Peter: *(firmly)* Rulers and elders of Israel, if you brought us here because we were kind to man who couldn't walk, I'll be glad to answer your questions. You ask how he was healed? Then know this: It is by the name of Jesus Christ of Nazareth that this man stands before you healed.

Healed Man: *(pumps fist in the air)* You tell 'em, Peter!

(John gives the healed man a hug.)

Annas: *(behind his hand, to the audience)* Look—they have no fear at all! They should be terrified of us.

Peter: This man was healed by Jesus' power. You crucified Jesus, but God raised him from the dead. Salvation is found in no one else. There is no other name under heaven by which we must be saved.

Annas: Leave the room!

Peter and John step back.

Annas: What can I do? These men aren't afraid of me. And everyone in Jerusalem has seen the great miracle they did. We'll have to order them not to speak of Jesus any more.

(Beckon Peter and John to return.)

Annas: You may not speak or teach in the name of Jesus anymore. We forbid it!

Peter: Judge for yourselves whether it's right for us to obey you or go obey God.

John: We can't help but tell about the things we've seen and heard.

Healed Man: *(to Peter and John)* You've been with Jesus from the beginning. And the Holy Spirit is with you now. Look—you healed me! It's the Holy Spirit who's given you courage to stand up to the Sanhedrin like this.

Annas: You'll stop preaching about Jesus now if you know what's good for you. We'll keep our eye on you. One more word about Jesus and you'll be back in jail. Now go!

(Annas backs away; Peter, John and the Healed Man move to the center.)

Peter: The Holy Spirit was with us. It was really God speaking through us.

John: Let's get back and tell the others what's happened.

Healed Man: *(as they exit)* You told 'em. You really told 'em!

That was quite a showdown! Annas and Peter had quite a bit to say to each other. Let's see how much of the story you caught!

Toss the four numbered balls to different parts of the room. Bring the kids with the balls to the front one-by-one and ask these questions. Allow kids to get help from the group if they need it. After each correct answer, let kids drop their balls into a bag.

■ **How did Peter and John end up in jail?**

■ **What was surprising about what Peter said to the members of the Sanhedrin?**

■ **Why didn't Peter and John just stand there and tremble in their sandals?**

■ **Has there been a time in your life when you spoke up for Jesus? When? Explain.**

Standing up for Jesus and his teachings was a pretty dangerous thing to do back in the days of the early church. Not only were Peter and John and the other apostles put in jail, they were also punished in other ways. They were made fun of and rejected by their friends and family. People threw rocks at them and spit on them. Some of the apostles were even killed because they kept on spreading the Gospel.

Yet, through it all, God was with them. The Holy Spirit gave them courage to stand up and tell the truth about Jesus to the very group of people who had called for Jesus' death. Do you know why? Because giving people the Good News about the Savior was even more important to Peter and John than life itself!

Bible Verse
But Peter and John replied, "We cannot help speaking about what we have seen and heard." Acts 4:20

You never know when God will give you a chance to speak out for him. Many people challenge God's truth today, just as they did all those years ago. When the time comes for you to speak out about your faith, you can count on the Holy Spirit to be with you just as he was with Peter and John.

Today in your shepherd groups you'll get a dose of courage from God's Word!

Dismiss kids to their shepherd groups.

② Shepherd's Spot

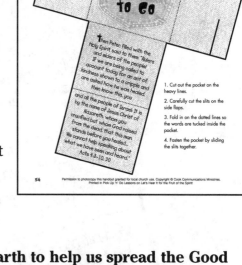

Gather your small group and help kids find Acts 4 in their Bibles.

Courtroom dramas are popular on TV. Today's Bible story unfolds a thrilling courtroom drama involving two of the most powerful figures of the early church—the apostles Peter and John. You may remember, they were two of Jesus' best friends. Let's read about their day in court straight from he book of Acts.

Have volunteers take turns reading Acts 4:1–13 aloud.

■ If you were a lawyer for Peter and John, what advice would you give them? Why would you say that?

■ What comment did the members of the court make about Peter and John? *(That they had been with Jesus.)*

Jesus prepared his disciples for times like this. Have a volunteer read Mark 13:11: "Whenever you are arrested and brought to trial, do not worry beforehand about what to say. Just say whatever is given you at the time, for it is not you speaking, but the Holy Spirit."

It happened just as Jesus promised! The Holy Spirit gave Peter and John the words to say. When it's your turn to speak out for Jesus, remember that the Holy Spirit will be with you as well. This cool little paper pocket will remind you of Jesus' promise and of Peter's bold speech.

Pass out the "Pocketful of Courage" handout. Have kids cut and fold it according to the directions on the handout.

■ Have you had the opportunity to speak out for Jesus? When do you think that might happen?

The Holy Spirit came to earth to help us spread the Good News about Jesus. Keep this little reminder in a special place so you'll remember that when you tell others about Jesus, the Holy Spirit is right there helping you know just what to say.

Invite kids to tell you about relatives and friends who need to hear the Good News about Jesus. Then close with prayer. **Lord, help us speak out for you just as Peter and John did in today's story. Thank you for the promise that your Holy Spirit will help us know what to say. We pray that you'll give us opportunities to tell** (mentioned people kids named) **about you. Give us the courage to be bold witnesses. We pray in Jesus' name, amen.**

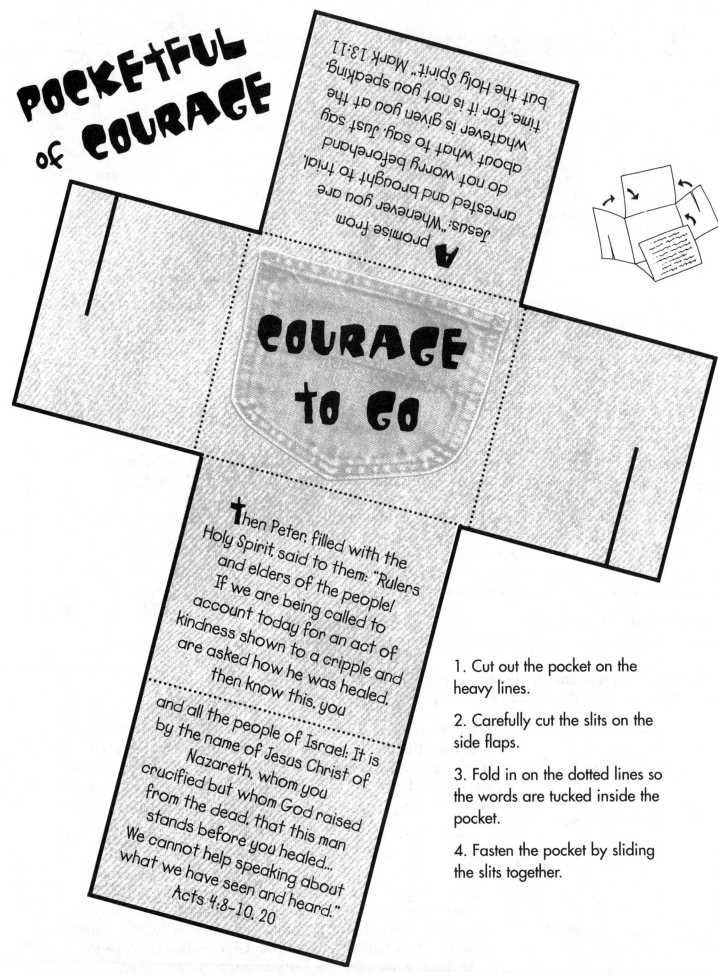

POCKETFUL of COURAGE

COURAGE TO GO

A promise from Jesus: "Whenever you are arrested and brought to trial, do not worry beforehand about what to say. Just say whatever is given you at the time, for it is not you speaking, but the Holy Spirit". Mark 13:11

✝ Then Peter, filled with the Holy Spirit, said to them: "Rulers and elders of the people! If we are being called to account today for an act of kindness shown to a cripple and are asked how he was healed, then know this, you and all the people of Israel: It is by the name of Jesus Christ of Nazareth, whom you crucified but whom God raised from the dead, that this man stands before you healed... We cannot help speaking about what we have seen and heard." Acts 4:8–10, 20

1. Cut out the pocket on the heavy lines.

2. Carefully cut the slits on the side flaps.

3. Fold in on the dotted lines so the words are tucked inside the pocket.

4. Fasten the pocket by sliding the slits together.

Workshop Wonders

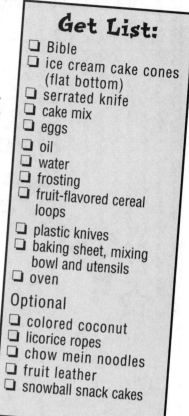
The members of the Sanhedrin didn't want to hear the truth about Jesus. They knew his power was for real. After all, the man Peter and John had healed was standing right in front of them. But they closed their hearts to the truth. Even though Peter and John had spent a not-so-pleasant night in a Jerusalem jail, they were determined and ready as ever to proclaim the truth that Jesus is the Son of God.

■ Peter and John went to jail for telling others about Jesus. How would you feel if someone you loved was sent to jail for telling the truth?

The priests and teachers of the Law threatened Peter and John, but the Holy Spirit was with the two apostles and helped them proclaim that Jesus was the Savior, come to free people from their sins. Use a serrated knife to saw off the bottom of an ice cream cone. Bring it to your lips and use it as a quick megaphone.

Hear ye! Hear ye! God's Spirit gives us courage to speak out for Jesus!

I have another use for our ice cream cones today. Let's make **Cone Head Buddies to celebrate the courage the Holy Spirit gives us to speak out.** Gather kids in the kitchen. Preheat the oven to 350°. Mix up a batch of cake batter following the instructions on the cake mix box. Have kids help line up the cake cones, one for each child in your class, on a baking sheet. Pour batter into the cones filling them halfway. Slip the tray into the oven and bake for 20 minutes until done.

As the treats bake, encourage kids to tell about times they've told others about Jesus. Ask them to think of situations at school when they might have a chance to speak out for Jesus, and to role-play how they would respond. You may want to tell some stories of your own. Remind them that we're not on our own—the Holy Spirit helps us tell others that Jesus is our savior and our Lord.

Cool the cones and frost. Use a dab of frosting to secure two cereal circle "eyes" and a mouth to the front of the cones. If you wish, use colored coconut, lengths of licorice or Chinese noodles for imaginative hairstyles for your cone head snacks. Add red fruit leather mouths that speak out for Jesus!

Read Acts 4:20: *"But Peter and John replied, 'We cannot help speaking about what we have seen and heard.'"*

As kids enjoy their cone head snacks, review what they've learned about the Holy Spirit. **Let's follow buddies Peter and John's example to speak out for Jesus. We've got the greatest news to share and God's Spirit to help us.**

Simpler Option: Let kids decorate ready-made snowball snack cakes placed on top of the ice cream cones.

Fold down the corners to start your paper airplane.

SPECIAL DELIVERY

TO

Speak out for Jesus.

Today at church we learned that God's spirit gives us courage to speak out for Jesus • Peter and John got sent to jail for healing a sick man and telling that they did it in Jesus' name. Have you ever been in trouble for doing the right thing? Tell about it.

Family FUN

Not having enough courage can certainly sink the ship! Try this experiment and see. Fill a glass with water. Drop in a carrot chunk. Watch what happens. (The carrots sinks.) Does this remind you of your courage in scary times? When we feel timid we can pray for the Holy Spirit's help to speak up for Jesus. Slowly sprinkle a tablespoon of salt into the water. Add another. Watch as your "courage" quickly rises to the surface.

Bible Verse

But Peter and John replied, "We cannot help speaking about what we have seen and heard."
Acts 4:20

Live It!

◇ If you could share lunch with Peter what would you ask him about courage?

◇ How do you get up the courage to tell the truth about Jesus? (The Holy Spirit helps you.)

◇ Does our family speak out for Jesus? How?

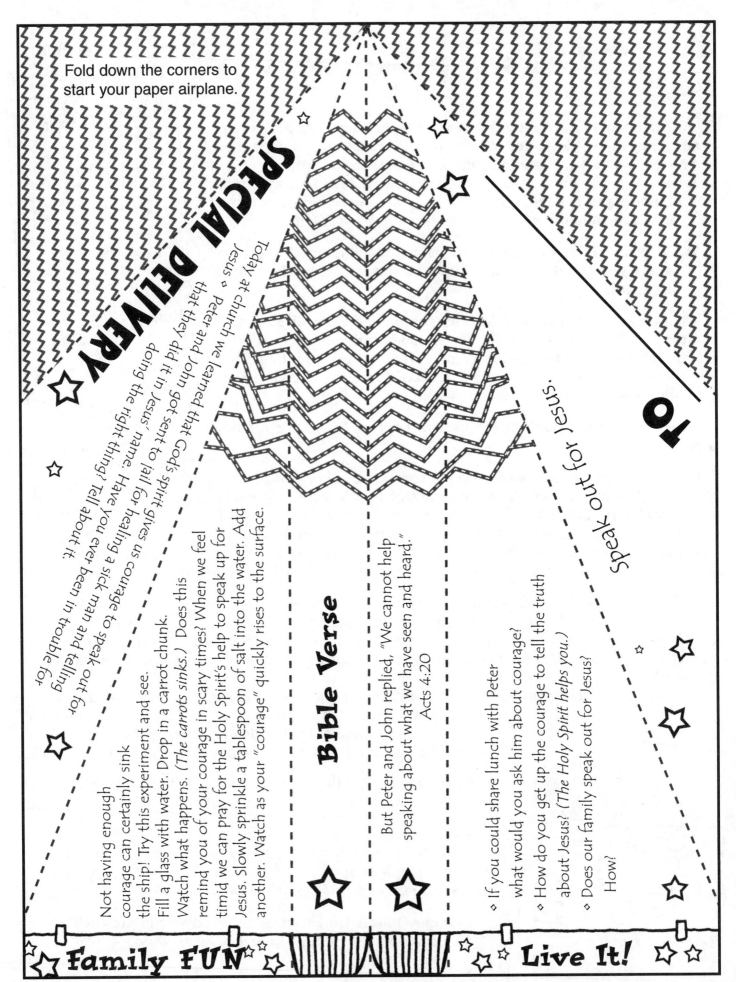

Ananias in Action

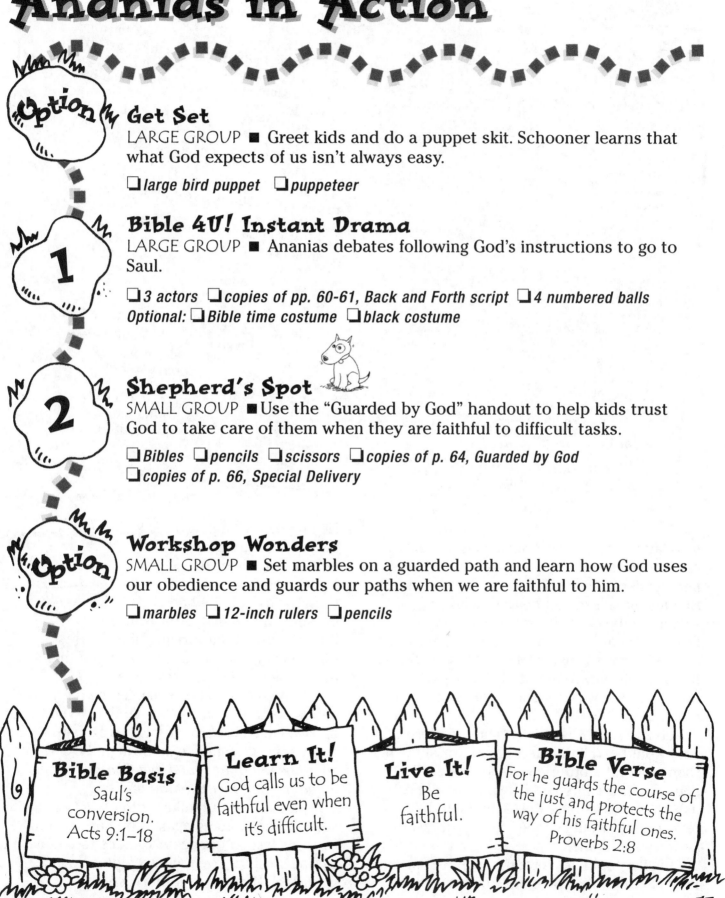

Get Set
LARGE GROUP ■ Greet kids and do a puppet skit. Schooner learns that what God expects of us isn't always easy.

❑ *large bird puppet* ❑ *puppeteer*

Bible 4U! Instant Drama
LARGE GROUP ■ Ananias debates following God's instructions to go to Saul.

❑ *3 actors* ❑ *copies of pp. 60-61, Back and Forth script* ❑ *4 numbered balls*
Optional: ❑ *Bible time costume* ❑ *black costume*

Shepherd's Spot
SMALL GROUP ■ Use the "Guarded by God" handout to help kids trust God to take care of them when they are faithful to difficult tasks.

❑ *Bibles* ❑ *pencils* ❑ *scissors* ❑ *copies of p. 64, Guarded by God*
❑ *copies of p. 66, Special Delivery*

Workshop Wonders
SMALL GROUP ■ Set marbles on a guarded path and learn how God uses our obedience and guards our paths when we are faithful to him.

❑ *marbles* ❑ *12-inch rulers* ❑ *pencils*

Bible Basis
Saul's conversion.
Acts 9:1–18

Learn It!
God calls us to be faithful even when it's difficult.

Live It!
Be faithful.

Bible Verse
For he guards the course of the just and protects the way of his faithful ones.
Proverbs 2:8

9:1 Meanwhile, Saul was still breathing out murderous threats against the Lord's disciples. He went to the high priest 2 and asked him for letters to the synagogues in Damascus, so that if he found any there who belonged to the Way, whether men or women, he might take them as prisoners to Jerusalem.

3 As he neared Damascus on his journey, suddenly a light from heaven flashed around him.

4 He fell to the ground and heard a voice say to him, "Saul, Saul, why do you persecute me?"

5 "Who are you, Lord?" Saul asked. "I am Jesus, whom you are persecuting," he replied.

6 "Now get up and go into the city, and you will be told what you must do."

7 The men traveling with Saul stood there speechless; they heard the sound but did not see anyone.

8 Saul got up from the ground, but when he opened his eyes he could see nothing. So they led him by the hand into Damascus.

9 For three days he was blind, and did not eat or drink anything.

10 In Damascus there was a disciple named Ananias. The Lord called to him in a vision, "Ananias!" "Yes, Lord," he answered.

11 The Lord told him, "Go to the house of Judas on Straight Street and ask for a man from Tarsus named Saul, for he is praying.

12 In a vision he has seen a man named Ananias come and place his hands on him to restore his sight."

13 "Lord," Ananias answered, "I have heard many reports about this man and all the harm he has done to your saints in Jerusalem.

14 And he has come here with authority from the chief priests to arrest all who call on your name."

15 But the Lord said to Ananias, "Go! This man is my chosen instrument to carry my name before the Gentiles and their kings and before the people of Israel.

16 I will show him how much he must suffer for my name."

17 Then Ananias went to the house and entered it. Placing his hands on Saul, he said, "Brother Saul, the Lord—Jesus, who appeared to you on the road as you were coming here—has sent me so that you may see again and be filled with the Holy Spirit."

18 Immediately, something like scales fell from Saul's eyes, and he could see again. He got up and was baptized,

Insights

Go lay hands on Saul? Ananias had plenty of reasons to raise an eyebrow—or two! Saul was fiercely dedicated to stamping out Christianity. He had witnessed Stephen's stoning and seemed to be eager for more of the same. From a human perspective, it must have been a relief to have Saul out of commission. Struck blind on his way to arrest Christians in Damascus, he was no longer very likely to do much harm.

But God had other plans. The transformed Saul would carry the message of Christ farther than any of the other apostles. He would speak to governors and kings. He would establish churches all over Asia Minor and his letters to them would encourage Christians for centuries to come.

Ananias could not have dreamed of the impact Paul's life would have on the church. He only knew Paul as a powerful Pharisee to be feared, someone so zealous against Christianity that he had obtained an official letter from the high priest authorizing him to arrest Christians from the region and bring them back to Jerusalem as prisoners.

Yet when God called Ananias to go lay his hands on Saul, Ananias faithfully obeyed. What must have gone through his head as he approached the house on Straight Street? *I've got to be out of my mind, but God has never failed me and I will not fail him now.*

It takes a faithful follower to obey God's will when it seems to go against human reason. Use this lesson to encourage kids to be faithful to God's calling even when common sense would tell them to do otherwise.

Get Set

Have a pad and pencil on hand. Open with praise songs, then greet the kids. **Hey—it's good to see your smiling faces! The words for today are: Be faithful! God wants us to faithfully obey him even when we think we know what's best. There's no such thing as being wiser than God, is there, Schooner?** *Schooner pops up.*

Schooner: *Squawk!* God is wiser than anyone. Even a birdbrain knows that.

Leader: I don't think you're such a birdbrain. As a matter of fact, I was going to ask you to help me with something today, Schooner.

Schooner: At your service, boss.

Leader: I'd like to make a bulletin board for our group.

Schooner: A bulletin board? Like where people advertise birdseed for sale?

Leader: Not exactly. But I think you'll like it.

Schooner: Can we use those fancy scissors that make fun paper shapes?

Leader: Sure.

Schooner: And how about those cut-away letters and sparkly 3-D stickers?

Leader: Yes, Schooner. But it's the purpose of the bulletin board that's most important.

Schooner: So clue me in. What's the purpose?

Leader: I want to put up some guidelines about how to treat each other.

Schooner: Class rules, huh? Like no dive-bombing or loud squawking during the story?

Leader: Those are good rules for parrots.

Schooner: Okay, so you want people rules. How about, *Be kind*?

Leader: *(writes on pad)* That's a good one. Be kind.

Schooner: Yes. Be kind...when others are kind to you.

Leader: Wait a minute...

Schooner: Rule #2: Be helpful.

Leader: *(writes on pad)* Okay...Be helpful.

Schooner: Be helpful...when others are helpful to you.

Leader: Schooner...

Schooner: Rule #3: Be faithful.

Leader: *(writes on pad)* Be faithful.

Schooner: Be faithful...if others treat you nice.

Leader: *(puts pad and pencil down)* Stop, Schooner. Stop. Stop. Stop.

Schooner: Why? I'm full of ideas today!

Leader: This isn't going the way I planned.

Schooner: Well, you did ask me for ideas.

Leader: I did. But you're only getting things half right.

Schooner: Which half? Be kind makes a great rule.

Leader: It does, Schooner. But anyone can be kind to people who are kind to them.

Schooner: Well, you wouldn't want it the other way around.

Leader: As a matter of fact, that's a lot like what God asked of a man in today's Bible story. His name was Ananias. God asked Ananias to take care of someone who was mean to God's people. Ananias wasn't too excited about it at first.

Schooner: I wouldn't be either. Why be kind to someone who isn't kind to begin with? That's dumb.

Leader: I thought you said no one was wiser than God.

Schooner: Well, yeah. I mean, um...God wouldn't ask us to be kind to someone who's mean. That just doesn't make sense.

Leader: God wants to faithfully obey him, no matter what he asks us to do. The Holy Spirit helps us to be faithful.

Schooner: But how can anybody...

Leader: On our own, we can't. But the Holy Spirit helps us handle even the hard things God asks us to do.

Schooner: Should we start over?

Leader: First, let's go to Bible 4U!.

Schooner: Goody! That's my favorite part. *Squawk!*

Welcome to another exciting day in Bible 4U! Today we're going to meet a man who had a tough choice to make. Ananias was a faithful Christian who lived in Damascus. God told Ananias to do a really hard thing. He wanted Ananias to help a man named Saul—a man whose number-one mission in life was to get rid of all the Christians he could find!

But God had other plans for Saul. God spoke to Saul when he was on his way to Damascus to arrest Christians.

Instant Prep

Before class, ask three volunteers to play the roles of A1, A2 and the Narrator. Give them copies of the "Back and Forth" script below. You may wish to take the Narrator's role yourself.

When God spoke, Saul fell to the ground, blind. Jesus himself spoke to Saul and told him to go into the city and wait.

That's where Ananias enters the picture. God chose Ananias to go pray for Saul so his sight would return, then help Saul take his first baby steps as a Christian. But how could Ananias trust a man like Saul? What if it was all a terrible trick?

for Overachievers

Have a three-person drama team prepare the story. Dress A1 in a Bible time costume and A2 in solid black. The Narrator can wear contemporary clothes. Create a backdrop of a simple Bibletime home.

Let's go ahead and meet Ananias and see what happened.

Back and Forth
Based on Acts 9:1–18

Narrator: Have you ever had an argument with yourself? There's a voice inside your head that wants you to do one thing and another voice that wants you to do something else. We're about to meet a man named Ananias, a Christian from Damascus, who's having one of those arguments with himself. Ananias is the kind of man you'd like to have for a friend, a man of prayer who's faithful to God in every circumstance. Let's welcome Ananias—his better half and his, well, not-so-good half.

(A1 and A2 enter, with A1 standing in front. When A2 speaks, he leans out from behind A1, first to the left side, then to the right.)

A1: Greetings in the name of the Lord! I'm Ananias.
A2: *(leans out from behind A1)* I'm Ananias too. You might say I'm his cautious side. *(Ducks back behind A1.)*
A1: I'm the part of Ananias that wants to serve God with all my heart.
A2: *(pops out)* I want to serve God too. But I know I have to look out for us.
A1: I know that I can trust God no matter what happens. My life is totally dedicated to serving him.

A2: But, you know, I have to remind us to use common sense.

A1: I feel so close to God when I pray. I feel so privileged that God has chosen me to serve him. *(Hesitates.)* Oh, my!

A2: What is it? What's up?

A1: God just spoke to me!

A2: Well, don't just stand there with your teeth in your mouth. What did he say?

A1: He wants me to go over to Straight Street and pray for Saul.

A2: Saul? God wants you to visit *the* Saul and pray for him?

A1: That's right. His directions were as plain as day.

A2: This wouldn't be Saul who has been making trouble for Christians, would it?

A1: The very one.

A2: Why does he need to be prayed for?

A1: He was coming here to arrest Christians and take them back to Jerusalem...

A2: So let's stay as far away from him as we can!

A1: But God spoke to him on the road. Knocked him down, as a matter of fact, and left him blind. He's waiting for me to come and pray for his sight to come back.

A2: But Saul being blind is a good thing! How can he arrest us if he can't even see us? I think we got a lucky break.

A1: I know it's hard to understand, but I'm supposed to go pray for him so his sight will come back.

A2: And then head for the hills before he arrests us? I don't think so.

A1: I'll admit that it doesn't seem to make a lot of sense, but God told me to go to him and I'm going to do it.

A2: Let's think through this. You could have gotten your wires crossed. Saul is the enemy of the church. There could be another Saul somewhere in town—a much nicer guy who isn't here to arrest Christians.

A1: God told me to go to Straight Street and pray for Saul and I'm going to be faithful to God's command.

A2: I can't believe this! Listen—I've got to talk some sense into you.

A1: God is wise and I trust him. I'm going to do what he says, no matter what.

A2: Don't you think you're taking this too seriously? I mean, God expects us to watch out for ourselves.

A1: There's no use arguing with me anymore. I'm leaving for Straight Street right now.

A2: I can't believe this. I really can't.

A1: There's a proverb that comes to mind.

A2: Great. I could use a good proverb about now.

A1: King Solomon said, "For he guards the course of the just and protects the way of his faithful ones."

A2: I vaguely remember that. It's Proverbs 2:8, isn't it?

A1: That's the one.

A2: So...you're determined to go through with this.

A1: By God's grace I'll be faithful to his command.

A2: Then there's no point in me saying anything else.

A1: No point at all.

A2: Then the best thing for me to do is give it up and fade into the background.

A1: Yep.

A2: Fine. Fine, fine, fine, fine, FINE! *(backs away.)*

A1: *(prayerfully)* Be with me, Lord. Help me do your will. *(Exits.)*

Narrator: Ananias had no way of knowing the wonderful things that would come of his visit to Saul. Saul became the apostle Paul, a powerful preacher and teacher who spread the Good News of Jesus far and wide. Paul's letters to churches became a big part of the New Testament. As a matter of fact, it was Paul who wrote about the fruit of the spirit! All this happened because Ananias remained faithful to God's command to pray for an enemy. Now it's your turn. Go—and faithfully serve the Lord your God! *(Exits.)*

Wow! Ananias really came through on a scary assignment. Let's toss around a few questions about this story. Toss the four numbered balls to different parts of the room.

Bring the kids with the balls to the front one-by-one and ask these questions. Allow kids to get help from the group if they need it. After each correct answer, let kids drop their balls into a bag.

 ■ **What surprising thing did God tell Ananias to do?**

 ■ **Why didn't these orders from God make sense at first?**

 ■ **Why do you think Ananias decided to obey God?**

 ■ **When is it tough for you to be faithful to God's commands?**

Ananias had no idea what a difference he was about to make in God's kingdom. He only knew who Saul was—a terrible enemy who was out to get as many of Jesus' followers as he could. When Ananias first got his marching orders from God, he must have been terribly confused. But he was faithful, because he knew that only God could see the whole picture.

Bible Verse
For he guards the course of the just and protects the way of his faithful ones.
Proverbs 2:8

It's not so hard to take risks when we know that God is in charge. His plans are always far beyond anything we can see or imagine. God relies on faithful people like Ananias and you and me to get with his program and do what he tells us to do. As we saw in today's story, even the smallest step of obedience can make a huge difference in God's kingdom. The Holy Spirit helps us remain faithful to God's commands. And he watches over us as well.

Today in your shepherd groups, you'll get to make a simple reminder of how God protects those who serve him faithfully.

 *Dismiss kids to their shepherd groups.*

2 Shepherd's Spot

Gather your small group and help kids find Acts 9 in their Bibles.

In today's Bible story we found out about someone who was about to make a big difference in God's kingdom. Saul started out as a super-bad guy—doing terrible things to all the Christians he could get his hands on. But God was about to change him, and he used a faithful Christian named Ananias to help bring about that change.

Have kids take turns reading Acts 9:1-19 aloud.

■ **Have you ever had an argument with yourself about whether or not to be faithful to God? How did that turn out?**

God wants us to know that he doesn't just give us a hard job and send us on our merry way. The Holy Spirit is our helper and counselor. He reminds us to be faithful, and he gives us the strength to do what God asks. Not only that, we're about to discover a wonderful scripture that assures us that God takes care of those who are faithful to him.

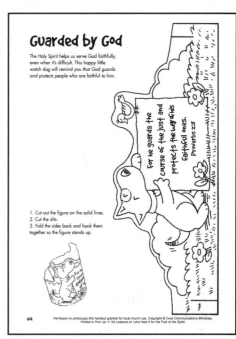

Pass out the "Guarded by God" handout. Ask a volunteer to read Proverbs 2:8 aloud.

This adorable little pooch would like you to take him home! He wants to sit on your dresser and remind you that when you're faithful to God, God guards and protects you. Have kids cut out the figure and fold back and hook the sides so it stands up.

■ **When is it most difficult for you to be faithful to what God asks you do to?**

■ **How does this verse encourage you?**

Let's pray for each other today. Invite kids to tell when they need God's help to be faithful. **Dear Lord, we're so thankful for people like Ananias who faithfully obey you. We want to be faithful to you too. Today I pray for** (name kids and the situations they shared). **Thank you for the Holy Spirit who helps us do hard things for you, and for watching over us as we live the way you want us to. In Jesus' name, amen.**

Guarded by God

The Holy Spirit helps us serve God faithfully, even when it's difficult. This happy little watch dog will remind you that God guards and protects people who are faithful to him.

1. Cut out the figure on the solid lines.
2. Cut the slits.
3. Fold the sides back and hook them together so the figure stands up.

For he guards the course of the just and protects the way of his faithful ones. Proverbs 2:8

Imagine how Ananias felt when he heard what God wanted him to do. *Gulp! Are you sure? You want me to go to Saul and do what? He kills people like me, Lord.* But God was not about to take no for an answer. Ananias would quickly come to the understanding that God was bigger than any threat Saul could make. God would protect him.

Get List:
- ❏ marbles
- ❏ 12-inch rulers
- ❏ pencils

Ananias was a follower of Jesus, a disciple. As a disciple, Ananias knew what God expected of him: faithfulness. Going to Saul was difficult but Ananias was faithful.

■ **A hateful Saul was God's "chosen instrument" (Acts 9:15) to do his will on earth. On a scale of 1 to 5, how hard was this for Ananias to understand?** *(Ananias questioned the wisdom of God. Imagine!)*

■ **What does God promise those who have faith in him and do his will?** *(That he will guard and protect them.)*

It isn't easy to be faithful when we don't understand or agree with what God wants from us. Easy or not, faithfulness is what God wants and he gives us the Holy Spirit to guide us.

Distribute two rulers and two pencils per child. Place the rulers on the table or floor so they are parallel to each other about two inches apart. Use the pencils to close off the rectangular ruler "box." Drop two marbles near the top of the box and the last one close to the opposite end.

The Bible is all about God. In it we find all of God's promises. Today's verse tells us about one of his promises. Let's say the verse together.

"For he guards the course of the just and protects the way of his faithful ones." Proverbs 2:8

■ **What happens when you feel scared about obeying God? How do you handle it?**

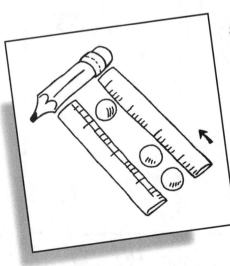

The Bible tells us that God guards our course, just as the rulers guide the marbles. Flick or roll one marble so it hits the second. Watch what happens. The motion of the first marble sets in motion the second which in turn hits the third. **When pressures come, God promises to protect our way. Our part is to stay faithful, to constantly follow God's direction.**

Our faithfulness sets in motion a chain of events similar to what happens with these marbles. With each step of obedience, God makes things happen for the good of his kingdom. That's why it's so important to listen to God and obey his commands, even if we don't really understand at first. Keep a favorite marble as a reminder to stay the course and trust God to guard your path.

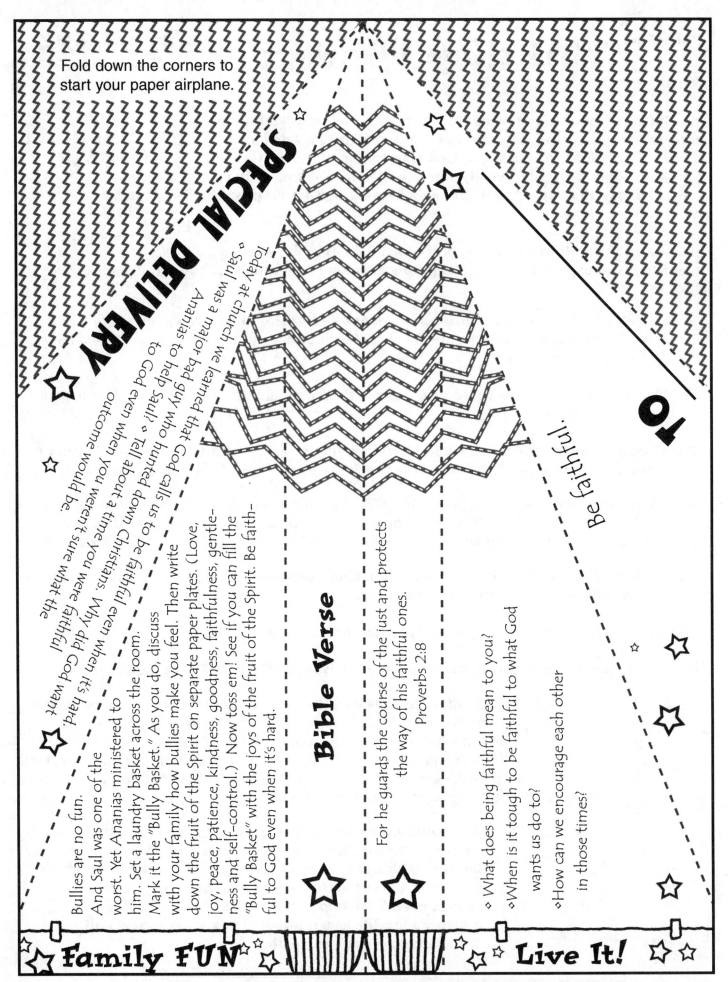

Fold down the corners to start your paper airplane.

SPECIAL DELIVERY

TO

Be faithful.

Today at church we learned that God calls us to be faithful even when it's hard. "Saul was a major bad guy who hunted down Christians. Why did God want to help Saul? Tell about a time you weren't sure what the outcome would be. Ananias ministered to him even when you weren't sure what the outcome would be.

Bullies are no fun. And Saul was one of the worst. Yet Ananias ministered to him. Set a laundry basket across the room. Mark it the "Bully Basket." As you do, discuss with your family how bullies make you feel. Then write down the fruit of the Spirit on separate paper plates. (Love, joy, peace, patience, kindness, goodness, faithfulness, gentleness and self-control.) Now toss 'em! See if you can fill the "Bully Basket" with the joys of the fruit of the Spirit. Be faithful to God even when it's hard.

Bible Verse

For he guards the course of the just and protects the way of his faithful ones.
Proverbs 2:8

◊ What does being faithful mean to you?
◊ When is it tough to be faithful to what God wants us do to?
◊ How can we encourage each other in those times?

Family FUN

Live It!

Barnabas At Bat

Option — Get Set

LARGE GROUP ■ Greet kids and do a puppet skit. Schooner learns that one person can change how a group thinks.

❑ large bird puppet   ❑ puppeteer

1 — Bible 4U! Instant Drama

LARGE GROUP ■ A father shares shocking news about Saul with his family.

❑ 3 actors ❑ copies of pp. 70–71, You Did What? script ❑ 4 numbered balls
Optional: ❑ Bibletime costumes ❑ Bibletime home set ❑ pottery dishes ❑ bread

2 — Shepherd's Spot

SMALL GROUP ■ Use the "Verse in a Frame" handout to give kids a visual reminder of how God expects us to respond to each other.

❑ Bibles ❑ pencils ❑ scissors ❑ copies of p. 74, Verse in a Frame
❑ copies of p. 76, Special Delivery

Option — Workshop Wonders

SMALL GROUP ■ Crepe paper teaches a fun and active lesson on gentleness.

❑ crepe paper rolls ❑ treats

Bible Basis
Barnabas goes to bat for Saul.
Acts 9:19–31

Learn It!
A gentle spirit brings people together.

Live It!
Be gentle.

Bible Verse
Be completely humble and gentle; be patient, bearing with one another in love.
Ephesians 4:2

Quick Takes

Acts 9:19–31

9:19 Saul spent several days with the disciples in Damascus.

20 At once he began to preach in the synagogues that Jesus is the Son of God.

21 All those who heard him were astonished and asked, "Isn't he the man who caused havoc in Jerusalem among those who call on this name? And hasn't he come here to take them as prisoners to the chief priests?"

22 Yet Saul grew more and more powerful and baffled the Jews living in Damascus by proving that Jesus is the Christ.

23 After many days had gone by, the Jews conspired to kill him,

24 but Saul learned of their plan. Day and night they kept close watch on the city gates in order to kill him.

25 But his followers took him by night and lowered him in a basket through an opening in the wall.

26 When he came to Jerusalem, he tried to join the disciples, but they were all afraid of him, not believing that he really was a disciple.

27 But Barnabas took him and brought him to the apostles. He told them how Saul on his journey had seen the Lord and that the Lord had spoken to him, and how in Damascus he had preached fearlessly in the name of Jesus.

28 So Saul stayed with them and moved about freely in Jerusalem, speaking boldly in the name of the Lord.

29 He talked and debated with the Grecian Jews, but they tried to kill him.

30 When the brothers learned of this, they took him down to Caesarea and sent him off to Tarsus.

31 Then the church throughout Judea, Galilee and Samaria enjoyed a time of peace. It was strengthened; and encouraged by the Holy Spirit, it grew in numbers, living in the fear of the Lord.

Insights

Who was this new Saul? Everyone was confused. This man who was known for his zealous persecution of Christians suddenly appeared in the synagogue in Damascus, arguing that Jesus is the Son of God. The Jews were dumbfounded. The Christians in Damascus who had personally discipled Saul were convinced that he was really a changed man. The Christians in Jerusalem, however, had their reservations. How could they believe the reports they were getting from Damascus? They had seen firsthand Saul's terrible persecution of Christians.

Christians from Damascus brought Saul to the apostles, but the reception was less than overwhelming. Even seeing him with their own eyes they doubted the sincerity of his faith in Christ. Up steps Barnabas, the Son of Encouragement. Mentioned in Acts 2 as one who sold his property and gave it to the disciples, Barnabas wielded a gentle, positive influence with great credibility. Barnabas vouched for Saul and managed to win the acceptance of the apostles for this up and coming evangelist.

It's impossible to underestimate the power of a godly, gentle encourager like Barnabas. His endorsement made all the difference in Saul's life. It turned him free to minister the Gospel to the known world. Use this lesson to encourage kids to see the best in people and to settle differences with a gentle spirit born of God.

Open with lively music, then greet the kids. **I think you'll like today's Bible story. It's about how a gentle man brings people together. His story teaches us that when we're patient and gentle it makes it a lot easier to love one another. Schooner, come join the fun!** *Schooner pops up.*

Leader: You know, Schooner, you pop up quite a bit when we're together.

Schooner: *(whispers to Leader)* It's written in the script, boss!

Leader: Pop ups remind me of baseball.

Schooner: It just so happens I used to coach baseball.

Leader: Oh really? What was the name of your team?

Schooner: The Red Wings, duh!

Leader: Be polite, Schooner.

Schooner: Sorry.

Leader: So you were the coach of the Red Wings?

Schooner: You bet I was.

Leader: Did you like being a coach?

Schooner: Most of the time.

Leader: When didn't you like it?

Schooner: *(sighs)* Once there was a tweet little Yellow Bird who wanted to be on the team.

Leader: And?

Schooner: Some of the other birds didn't want her. They said she was too small. So I said I'd put her in right field.

Leader: That was a wise move. You can go for inning after inning with not much happening in right field. Did they go for that?

Schooner: Nope. They said her wing was too weak.

Leader: That put you in a tough spot.

Schooner: It really did. I thought Yellow Bird had as much right to be on the team as anyone else. But I was the only one who did.

Leader: Sounds like she didn't make the team.

Schooner: *(brightening)* Oh, but she did!

Leader: She did? How?

Schooner: I took the other team members aside. I told them how I'd seen Yellow Bird catching pop flies with the Little Bird League. She was really good!

Leader: What happened then?

Schooner: They agreed to give her a try. Our shortstop got injured so I pulled her to the infield.

Leader: Wow, Schooner—you really went to bat for Yellow Bird.

Schooner: And she turned out to be great!

Leader: That's exactly like what happens in today's Bible story. Someone wanted to join with the early church and most folks didn't want him to. His name was Saul.

Schooner: Did Saul have a weak wing?

Leader: He was strong in every way. Trouble is, he'd used his strength to be really mean to Christians.

Schooner: Well, that's a foul ball.

Leader: But God had changed him. And a special person named Barnabas believed him and went to bat for him.

Schooner: Cool. Just like what I did for Yellow Bird. I like this guy. What's his name again?

Leader: Barnabas.

Schooner: I bet he waved his bat and said, "You'd better let Saul on this team or you'll be sorry!"

Leader: Nope. Barnabas was a gentle man. Because of his Christ-like spirit, he coached the others to accept Saul.

Schooner: So did Saul turn out to be an all-star?

Leader: Oh boy, did he! He even wrote several books of the Bible.

Schooner: Whoa—that gives me parrotbumps.

Leader: Don't you mean goosebumps?

Schooner: Do I look like a goose to you?

Leader: No, but I bet you'd like to hear more about his Bible story.

Schooner: I sure would!

Leader: Bible 4U! up nest, oops, I mean, *next!*

I have a feeling things are going to be a little bit tense in today's Bible 4U!. Why? It's been a few weeks since Saul, a terrible enemy of Christians, became a Christian himself. He studied and prayed with the Christians in Damascus. Then it was time to bring the new Saul to Jerusalem where he could meet with the church leaders.

Instant Prep
Before class, ask three volunteers to play the roles of Anna and Abner and their teenage daughter Sarah. Give them copies of the "You Did What?" script below to review.

You can imagine that the church leaders felt a pretty unpleasant jolt when they saw Saul standing in their midst. Was this a trick? Was he disguising himself as a Christian so he could arrest them all? No one was ready to give Saul the time of day—at least no one but Barnabas. Barnabas could see that Saul had changed big-time. He truly was a disciple of Jesus—one who could play a very important role in God's kingdom. So Barnabas spoke up for Saul.

for Overachievers
Have a three-person drama team prepare the story. Create a backdrop of a simple Bibletime home.

Let's see what happened when Abner, a man who met with the apostles, went home that night and told his family.

You Did What?
Based on Acts 9:19-31

Anna and Sarah enter and set out bowls on a low table.

Anna: I can't wait for your father to get home. You know, he met with the apostles today.

Sarah: What apostles?

Anna: Oi, Sarah. Where is your head? All you ever think about is boys! Jesus' apostles, the church leaders here in Jerusalem.

Sarah: Oh, those apostles. That's a big deal, huh?

Anna: Yes! The very men who walked with Jesus meet with the other leaders. They do all kinds of important things.

Sarah: Like what?

Anna: Like leading the church exactly the way Jesus would want them to. Reminding everyone of the Lord's teachings. Taking good care of God's people.

Abner enters.

Abner: Honey, I'm home!

Anna and Sarah take turns hugging him.

Anna: Shalom, my husband.

Sarah: Shalom, Papa.

Abner: I bless God that he has given me two such beautiful ladies in my house. More kisses for Papa.

They kiss him on each cheek.

Anna: What of your day, Abner? Was the Lord's brother there?

Abner: All the apostles were. And you would never believe who showed up.

Sarah: Who, Papa? Tell us!

Abner: Saul of Tarsus.

Anna: What? Was he there to arrest you? Are you all right?

Sarah: Who's Saul of Tarsus?

Anna: He's someone you want to stay far away from. He's a Pharisee. And he's made it his personal mission to hurt Christians.

Sarah: Was he there to spy on you, Papa?

Abner: No, he was there to join us!

Sarah and Anna: WHAT?

Abner: Saul has become a believer. Jesus spoke to him when he was on his way to Damascus to persecute the Christians there. He was struck blind, but Ananias laid hands on him and prayed for him. Now he can see again, and he's been preaching about Jesus.

Sarah: Are you sure it wasn't some kind of trick?

Abner: We weren't sure. When I saw Saul, I wanted to run right out the back door. Some of the apostles were angry until Barnabas straightened them out.

Sarah: Barnabas? I remember Barnabas!

Anna: *(to Abner)* Thank goodness the girl remembers something besides the good-looking son of the butcher.

Abner: What do you remember about Barnabas, my sweet?

Sarah: When you were out of work because nobody would hire Christians, Barnabas sold his land and gave the money to the apostles. And they used part of that money to help us.

Anna: God be praised for the help Barnabas gave to many of us!

Sarah: So what did Barnabas have to say?

Abner: That Saul believes in Jesus! That he's preached to many people and helped them find faith in the Lord too.

Sarah: That can't be. He's our enemy. You should have thrown him out.

Abner: That's what we thought at first. People were furious with Barnabas for bringing him.

Anna: I should think so!

Abner: But Barnabas gently explained.

Anna: Were you born yesterday that you would let a snake like Saul into the church?

Abner: Do you doubt the word of Barnabas?

Anna: Well, no, but...

Abner: Barnabas explained how God himself changed Saul, who's now known as Paul, by the way.

Anna: Barnabas is a man of God. Still, Saul got my cousin's family thrown in jail. If I saw him in the street, I'd give him a piece of my mind and throw in a black eye to boot.

Sarah: You go, Mama!

Abner: *(clears throat)* Doesn't God call us to be gentle people, Anna?

Anna: *(sighs)* You're right. I'm sorry. It's just that he's hurt so many people. I'll have to ask God to change my heart.

Abner: That he will do if you ask him.

Anna: Then that is what I must do! Thank you, my husband. *Family embraces.*

They exit.

I'm glad Abner finally got his supper! While the family chats, let's see how good you were at **eavesdropping on their conversation.** Toss the four numbered balls to different parts of the room.

Bring the kids with the balls to the front one by one and ask these questions. Allow kids to get help from the group if they need it. After each correct answer, let kids drop their balls into a bag.

 ■ **What was the Jerusalem council? What did it do?**

 ■ **Why were people in the council upset about seeing Saul there?**

 ■ **Why did Barnabas speak up for Saul?**

 ■ **Did you ever have anyone stick up for you? What was that like?**

Barnabas had a chance to spend some time with Saul, so he knew that the change in him was for real. But he also understood the anger and fear he saw in people's eyes when Saul showed up at a meeting of the apostles.

Bible Verse
Be completely humble and gentle; be patient, bearing with one another in love.
Ephesians 4:2

When the men of the church council wanted to send Saul away, Barnabas could have gotten angry and yelled, "Whatsamatta with you people? Don't you believe the power of God could change this man?" But an angry spirit usually makes a bad situation worse.

Instead, Barnabas gently explained that Jesus had spoken to Saul and that Saul had preached about Jesus in Damascus. The gentle spirit of Barnabas carried the day, and the apostles accepted Saul. Right away Saul began to preach so boldly that some of the religious leaders tried to put him to death. But that's another story!

Today in your shepherd groups, you'll get to see what it's like to bring people together with a gentle spirit.

 *Dismiss kids to their shepherd groups.*

② Shepherd's Spot

Gather your small group and help kids find Acts 9:19–31 in their Bibles.

This story takes place when the early church is growing like crazy. Christians have spread out from Jerusalem where people like Saul have made life very difficult for them. Who would have expected that Saul would meet God and have his life turned around? The Jews wanted to kill him and the Christians were afraid he wasn't for real. Some amazing things happened in this story that we didn't even have a chance to talk about. Listen for Saul's great escape as we read from the Bible.

Have volunteers take turns reading Acts 9:19-31 aloud.

■ **How did Saul get out of town?** *(His friends lowered him over the city wall in a basket at night.)*

■ **Why was Saul at the center of so many problems?**

■ **How do you think Barnabas knew that Saul was for real?**

Barnabas was in tune with the Holy Spirit. He had God's assurance that Saul was the real deal—an honest-to-goodness believer in Jesus. God used Barnabas's gentle spirit to smooth the way for Saul to be accepted in the church and begin a ministry that would bring thousands of people to faith in Jesus.

When we face conflict like Barnabas faced that day with the church leaders, a gentle spirit isn't always what comes to the forefront!

It's a good thing we have the Holy Spirit as our counselor. Paying attention to the voice of God makes a positive difference in how we respond. Distribute the "Verse in a Frame" handout. **This verse will help us stay on track!** Have a volunteer read Ephesians 4:2 aloud: *"Be completely humble and gentle; be patient, bearing with one another in love."*

Help kids fold the verse frame according to the instructions on the handout. Talk about where they can display the verse and share it with their families.

Invite kids to share prayer concerns, then close with prayer.

Verse in a Frame

Can you live up to the challenge of this verse? Only with the Holy Spirit's help! Fold the frame around the verse and display it where it will be a reminder to everyone in your family that a gentle spirit brings people together.

1. Cut out the frame on the heavy lines.
2. Fold the top and bottom back on the dotted lines.
3. Fold the sides back on the inner dotted lines.
4. Fold the sides forward on the inside edge of the border.

Be completely HUMBLE and GENTLE; be PATIENT, bearing with one another in love. Ephesians 4:2

Workshop Wonders

At the beginning of today's story, Saul was a hated outsider. His Christian friends from Damascus took him to the apostles in Jerusalem, but they wanted to turn him away. They knew about the terrible things Saul had done to Christians and they didn't trust him at all.

Get List:
❏ crepe paper rolls
❏ treats

Enter Barnabas with his gentle ways. He used his humble spirit to draw both sides together. With humility and patience he convinced the disciples that Saul was not someone to be feared or hated. His new ways were not his old ways. Almighty God had seen to that.

Let's play a game that will bring to life the characters of today's Bible story. The game is called "Connect!" and gentleness will help each team finish the game. Form trios. Within your trios, decide who is Barnabas, who is the Council and who is Saul. Give each Barnabas a ten-foot length of crepe paper. Crepe paper is delicate and easy to tear. The crepe paper will represent the humble and gentle spirit needed to bring and keep people together.

Now form a triangle in your teams with your backs to each other. It's the job of Barnabas, the gentle people connecter, to tie your ankles together with the crepe paper. Pause as each trio accomplishes this task.

When I say "Go!" your team needs to work together to move all the way around the room and back to your original spot. Barnabas is the coach. If you break your crepe paper ties, go back to your starting place. Barnabas will come to me for more crepe paper and you'll start over. When everyone finishes, we can share a yummy treat.

Gather kids and hand out treats.

■ Have you ever brought two sides together? What did you do or say to calm fears?

■ What did you learn about the power of gentleness?

■ How can you use what you learned in your life this week?

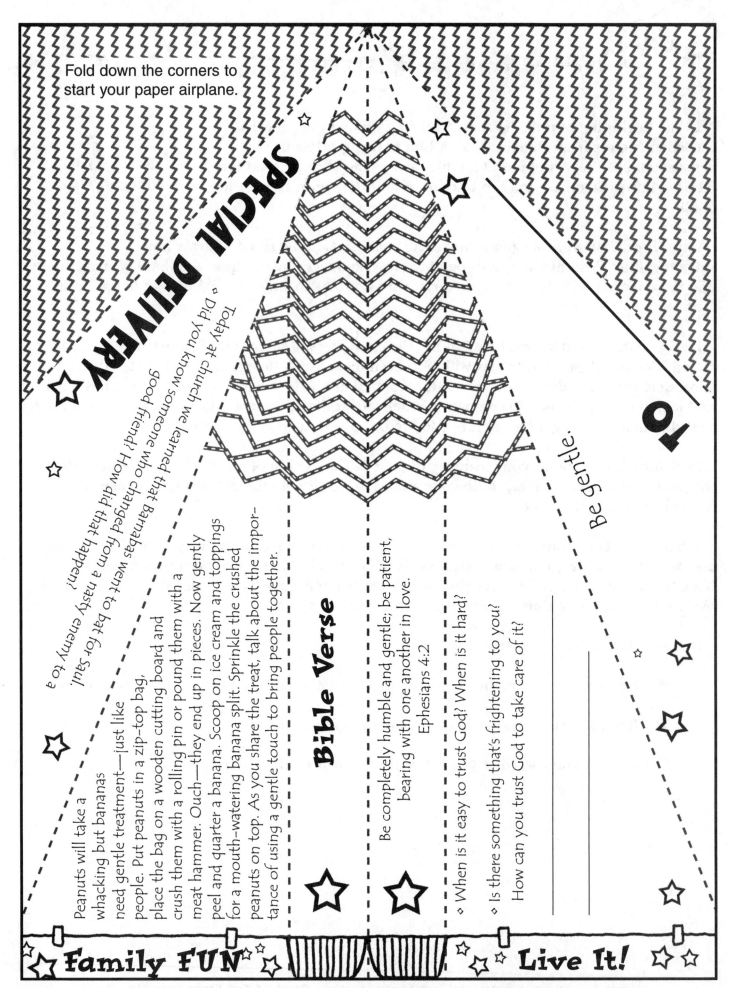

Fold down the corners to start your paper airplane.

SPECIAL DELIVERY

TO

Be gentle.

Today at church we learned that Barnabas went to bat for Saul. Did you know someone who changed from a nasty enemy to a good friend? How did that happen?

Family FUN

Peanuts will take a whacking but bananas need gentle treatment—just like people. Put peanuts in a zip-top bag, place the bag on a wooden cutting board and crush them with a rolling pin or pound them with a meat hammer. Ouch—they end up in pieces. Now gently peel and quarter a banana. Scoop on ice cream and toppings for a mouth-watering banana split. Sprinkle the crushed peanuts on top. As you share the treat, talk about the importance of using a gentle touch to bring people together.

Bible Verse

Be completely humble and gentle; be patient, bearing with one another in love.
Ephesians 4:2

Live It!

◇ When is it easy to trust God? When is it hard?

◇ Is there something that's frightening to you? How can you trust God to take care of it?

_____

_____

Peter Escapes from Prison

Option

Get Set
LARGE GROUP ■ Greet kids and do a puppet skit. Schooner tells about a bad dream about being caught in a cage.

❏ large bird puppet   ❏ puppeteer

1

Bible 4U! Instant Drama
LARGE GROUP ■ Set the stage for Peter, an angel and two imaginary guards.

❏ 4 actors   ❏ copies of pp. 80-81, Am I Dreaming? script   ❏ 4 numbered balls
Optional: ❏ prison cell set   ❏ Roman armor   ❏ two gates that open   ❏ Bibletime costumes

2

Shepherd's Spot
SMALL GROUP ■ Use the "Peace to You!" handout to help kids offer their fearful thoughts to God.

❏ Bibles   ❏ pencils   ❏ scissors   ❏ copies of p. 84, Peace to You! handout
❏ copies of p. 86, Special Delivery

Option

Workshop Wonders
SMALL GROUP ■ Make food figures that recreate scenes from the Bible story. Remind kids that they can be at peace because God is in control.

❏ paper plates   ❏ pretzel sticks   ❏ gumdrops   ❏ large marshmallows   ❏ Bible
Optional ❏ mini-marshmallows

Bible Basis
Peter escapes from prison.
Acts 12:6–18

Learn It!
God has everything under control.

Live It!
Be at peace and trust God.

Bible Verse
Do not be anxious about anything, but in everything, by prayer and petition, with thanksgiving, present your requests to God.
Philippians 4:6

Acts 12:6-18

12:6 The night before Herod was to bring him to trial, Peter was sleeping between two soldiers, bound with two chains, and sentries stood guard at the entrance.
7 Suddenly an angel of the Lord appeared and a light shone in the cell. He struck Peter on the side and woke him up. "Quick, get up!" he said, and the chains fell off Peter's wrists.
8 Then the angel said to him, "Put on your clothes and sandals." And Peter did so. "Wrap your cloak around you and follow me," the angel told him.
9 Peter followed him out of the prison, but he had no idea that what the angel was doing was really happening; he thought he was seeing a vision.
10 They passed the first and second guards and came to the iron gate leading to the city. It opened for them by itself, and they went through it. When they had walked the length of one street, suddenly the angel left him.
11 Then Peter came to himself and said, "Now I know without a doubt that the Lord sent his angel and rescued me from Herod's clutches and from everything the Jewish people were anticipating."

12 When this had dawned on him, he went to the house of Mary the mother of John, also called Mark, where many people had gathered and were praying.
13 Peter knocked at the outer entrance, and a servant girl named Rhoda came to answer the door.
14 When she recognized Peter's voice, she was so overjoyed she ran back without opening it and exclaimed, "Peter is at the door!"
15 "You're out of your mind," they told her. When she kept insisting that it was so, they said, "It must be his angel."
16 But Peter kept on knocking, and when they opened the door and saw him, they were astonished.
17 Peter motioned with his hand for them to be quiet and described how the Lord had brought him out of prison. "Tell James and the brothers about this," he said, and then he left for another place.
18 In the morning, there was no small commotion among the soldiers as to what had become of Peter.

Insights

The situation could hardly be worse. Herod had one of the apostles, James the brother of John, put to death. This act of arbitrary cruelty to Christians pushed Herod up several percentage points in the opinion polls with his biggest contingent—the Jews. Following the "if a little is good, more is better" philosophy, Herod went after Peter next. Peter had been the main mouthpiece of the church since the day of Pentecost. Shutting him down should please the Jews so much that it would be smooth sailing for Herod for months to come.

It's not hard to imagine how the Christians felt. They had just lost James—one of Jesus' closest friends. Now Peter lay chained in prison awaiting Herod's whim. The eleven who had been with Jesus were precious to the early believers. It was a terrible loss to see them cut down.

As desperate as the situation looked from a human perspective, God was not fazed by Herod's evil plans. The church prayed as Peter waited in prison to appear before Herod. Knowing of Peter's miracles, Herod surrounded him with an extraordinary number of guards—to no avail! An angel awakened Peter and led him right out of prison without Peter himself even realizing what was happening. When he arrived at the house where his friends were praying, they literally couldn't believe their eyes. God's deliverance shocked everyone.

It's humanly impossible to know peace in the midst of life-threatening circumstances. But Peter obviously knew God's peace. Use this lesson to teach kids that peace in the midst of terrible circumstances is a gift that only God can give.

Get Set

Open with lively music, then greet the kids. **Hello everyone!** *(Schooner makes a sobbing sound)* **Today we're going to talk about...***(Schooner sobs again)***...we're going to talk about being at peace because...** *(another huge sob from Schooner)* **What could be ailing that bird? Schooner, what's going on?** *Schooner pops up...sobbing!*

Schooner: *(sobs on Leader's shoulder)* Oh, it was so awful!

Leader: *(pats Schooner on the head)* What in the world happened, Schooner?

Schooner: It w-was a cage—a great big cage!

Leader: I don't see a cage anywhere.

Schooner: But it was there. And it tried to swallow me! *(sobs loudly)*

Leader: Calm down, Schooner. Take a deep breath and tell me what happened.

Schooner: I had a nightmare. But it felt so real.

Leader: Sometimes it helps to talk about it. Let's hear what's troubling you.

Schooner: You're a really sweet guy, boss. *(gives him a big smack on the cheek)*

Leader: *(rubs his cheek)* I don't think I've ever been beaked before. So tell me about your dream.

Schooner: Well, it started off being a really beautiful day and I decided to go for a little flight around the block.

Leader: But in real life you never leave our garden, do you?

Schooner: Never! I'm safe here and this is where I belong.

Leader: I'm glad you remember that.

Schooner: In my dream I was sailing around, catching up on what was happening with all the neighbors.

Leader: And then somebody saw a beautiful parrot.

Schooner: Yeah! And they waved a shiny plate full of seeds at me.

Leader: So, of course, you had to take a closer look.

Schooner: I dived for the plate of seeds, and the next thing I knew I was inside a CAGE!

Leader: You must've been frightened.

Schooner: Right—I got away. Just as the cage door was swinging shut, a big gust of wind blew it back. I made a quick escape...and then I woke up.

Leader: And here you are, safe and sound.

Schooner: I don't like to be locked up.

Leader: Being locked up is pretty scary. Just ask Peter.

Schooner: Who's Peter—another parrot?

Leader: No, he was a disciple of Jesus.

Schooner: And someone put him in a cage?

Leader: In a jail cell, actually, with guards all around him.

Schooner: Was he a bad bird, boss?

Leader: No way! Peter was a fine man—one of Jesus' closest friends.

Schooner: Then why was he a jailbird?

Leader: Because the king wanted to hurt him, just as he had hurt other Christians.

Schooner: Peter must've been scared out of his feathers!

Leader: I don't think he was, Schooner. He knew God was in control, so he fell asleep lying chained between two guards.

Schooner: Did they snore?

Leader: Peter didn't stick around to find out.

Schooner: Really? He got away? How?

Leader: I guess you'll find out in Bible 4U!

Schooner: What are we waiting for? Bible 4U! straight ahead!

1 Bible 4U!

Welcome back to Bible 4U! Do you remember our last story about Peter? He was in jail then, too. He spoke boldly about Jesus to the religious leaders in the Sanhedrin. They warned him never to preach about Jesus again, but Peter had to keep on telling about all the wonderful things Jesus had done.

The religious leaders never left Peter alone after that. So when Herod arrested Peter and kept him in jail, they were pretty happy. Herod had killed other Christian leaders, and Jesus' followers were pretty worried that he might do the same thing to Peter.

Peter's friends got together and prayed the whole time Peter was in prison. Things seemed pretty hopeless, but Peter's friends knew that God was greater than any mean old king, so they kept on praying. Then one night, Peter had an amazing dream—or so he thought…

Instant Prep

Before class, ask two kids to play the roles of Peter and the angel. Invite volunteers to play the non-speaking roles of guards and Christians who are praying. Give them copies of the "Am I Dreaming?" script below. Station two guards by Peter and two others beside an imaginary gate.

for Overachievers

Create a set that suggests a Roman prison. On the opposite side of the stage prepare a door to a house. Use real or paper chains to suggest that Peter is chained to two guards. Station sets of costumed guards at two imaginary gates. Use extras to portray the Christians praying for Peter.

Am I Dreaming?
Based on Acts 12:6-18

Peter is lying on the floor sleeping between two guards. After a few moments, he starts to toss and turn then looks out at the kids.

Peter: *(yawning)* What time is it? Where am I? *(looks around)* Oh yeah, prison. King Herod has been keeping me here for days, but they say tomorrow's my trial. To be honest, things don't look too good for me. The religious leaders would be happy if Herod decided to put me to death.

A soldier snores, then Peter crawls between the soldiers to get closer to the kids.

Peter: Do you know what my "crime" is? Teaching about Jesus. The Sanhedrin warned me months ago to stop, but I wasn't about to! God has used me and all the other apostles to do great miracles and bring the Good News about Jesus to thousands of people.

One of the guards snorts and rolls over in a comical position.

Peter: Just a few days ago Herod, our less-than-wonderful king, put James to death. What a loss! I think he has something similar planned for me. It would certainly make the religious leaders happy. You probably think

I'm scared out of my mind. Well, here's a piece of news for you: I'M NOT! The whole church is praying for me. Herod may have me surrounded by guards, but they're nothing compared to the living God! Who knows what will happen at my trial tomorrow? I can tell you this: no matter how things look, God is in control. My heart is at peace. *(yawns widely)* I'd better get some Zs. Tomorrow is a big day.

Peter lies down and begins to snore lightly. The angel enters, illuminated by a spot or several flashlights. He taps Peter on the side.

Peter: What…huh? Is it morning already? *(rubs his eyes then opens them)* Who lit all the torches? *(gasps as he sees the angel)* Am I dreaming, or are you an…

Angel: Quick! Get up and get your clothes on!

Peter jumps up right away and his chains fall off. He falls forward and nearly crashes into the angel.

Peter: Oops…sorry. Didn't realize the chains had fallen off.

Angel: Get your cloak on—quickly!

Peter immediately puts on his coat.

Peter: Ready.

Angel: Follow me.

Peter: But the guards. Besides these two there are…

Angel approaches guards by the gate and waves his hands in front of their faces. They stare straight ahead, unaware that anyone is there.

Peter: Is this a dream? *(pinches himself)* Ouch! Hmm…could this really be happening? Gates opening, guards acting as if we're not here?

Angel beckons for Peter to follow. Peter looks around as he walks, breathing deeply. The angel silently backs out of the scene.

Peter: Ahh! The streets of Jerusalem. The smells of the market—sweet, juicy fruit…fragrant perfumes…and my favorite smell: fresh fish. Wonder what the catch of the day might be—you got any idea?

Turns to the angel for an answer, but the angel is gone.

Peter: *(to kids)* Hey! Where'd he go? He was just here. I promise, there was a guy right here with me. He led me out of prison, and then…Hey, wait a minute. He led me out of prison? He led me out of prison! It really is a miracle. I'm out of prison, and God must have sent that angel to lead me out! The church has got to hear about this!

Peter takes off running.

Peter: *(panting)* There's the house where everyone is praying.

Peter pantomimes knocking on a door. Rhoda pretends to peek out, then backs up with her mouth covered in shock. She gestures wildly and several join her. They stand staring at Peter.

Peter: It's me! I know it's too good be true, but it's me!

The Christians embrace Peter.

Peter: See what your prayers have done? God sent an angel right into my prison cell. The guards didn't see or hear a thing as the angel led me out of prison. The hand of God opened the gates to let me out. At first I thought it was all a dream, but here I am!

The Christians praise God as Peter turns to the audience.

Peter: It looked like I was a goner, but God had everything under control. That's why I wasn't worried, even chained in prison. When it seems like everything is going bad, keep trusting in God. Let his peace fill your heart. He's greater than anything you can imagine, and you are precious to him. God's peace to you, my friends!

All exit.

All those people were gathered to pray for Peter, then BINGO—he was standing right there in front of them! God's power freed Peter from prison and the whole crisis was over before anyone had a clue what was going on. Let's see if you have a clue about what happened in this amazing story.

Toss the four numbered balls to different parts of the room. Bring the kids with the balls to the front one-by-one and ask these questions. Allow kids to get help from the group if they need it. After each correct answer, let kids drop their balls into a bag.

■ How could Peter sleep peacefully the night before his trial?

■ Although Peter followed all the angel's instructions, he didn't really realize what was happening until he was outside the prison. Why do you think God kept him "in the dark" until then?

■ You're one of the believers praying for Peter. What's your first reaction when Rhoda says he's at the door?

■ The church prayed faithfully for Peter. What situations do you know of that we need to be praying about?

The morning after the angel led Peter out of prison, Herod's soldiers were totally confused. Peter was gone, and they had no idea what had happened. Herod was seriously displeased, but the church was rejoicing. God had everything under control all along!

Imagine how worried everyone must have been. What would they do without Peter? They knew no one could stop Herod. No one but God, that is! Worry and fear come to us naturally. That's when need to remember, "God has everything under control. I don't know the outcome, but God does!" Then ask God to fill your heart with the peace that only he can give. So, the next time you're worried, what are you going to do? *Pause for kids to respond.*

Bible Verse
Do not be anxious about anything, but in everything, by prayer and petition, with thanksgiving, present your requests to God. Philippians 4:6

That's right—pray! Trusting God is the very best thing you can do. Today in your shepherd groups, you'll discover how the Holy Spirit fills your heart with peace when you trust God.

Dismiss kids to their shepherd groups.

2 Shepherd's Spot

Gather your small group and help kids find Acts 12 in their Bibles.

There's nothing quite as wonderful as a daring middle-of-the-night escape, is there? Especially when it involves an angel, gates that open by themselves, guards who don't see a thing and a nasty king who doesn't have a clue what happened! Let's read this story right from God's Word and make sure we don't miss a single exciting detail!

Have volunteers take turns reading Acts 12:6–18 aloud.

■ **Did you ever experience a time when you thought, "Man, things couldn't get any worse than this?"** Allow kids to share.

That's exactly what it looked like for Peter in this story. If I'd been there, I'd probably have been shaking in my sandals. But God doesn't want us to be scared. He wants to fill us with his peace. That's what today's verse is all about.

Pass out the "Peace to You!" handout. Invite a volunteer to read Philippians 4:6, 7 aloud: *"Do not be anxious about anything, but in everything, by prayer and petition, with thanksgiving, present your requests to God. And the peace of God, which transcends all understanding, will guard your hearts and your minds in Christ Jesus."* Have kids fold the rainbow figure in half and cut it out on the solid lines. Fold the bottom tabs forward so it stands up.

When worry and fear fill our hearts, it's hard to know God's peace. That's why he doesn't want us to keep everything to ourselves—he wants us to pray about it and share it with him. In prayer, you can dump your heavy load of worries. Then the Holy Spirit floods your heart with peace that's beyond anything we can understand.

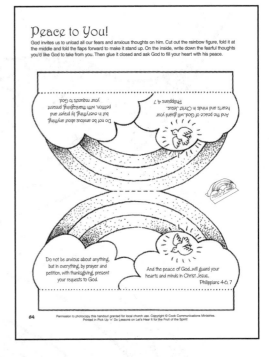

Peace to You!

God invites us to unload all our fears and anxious thoughts on him. Cut out the rainbow figure, fold it at the middle and fold the flaps forward to make it stand up. On the inside, write down the fearful thoughts you'd like God to take from you. Then glue it closed and ask God to fill your heart with his peace.

Do not be anxious about anything, but in everything, by prayer and petition, with thanksgiving, present your requests to God.

And the peace of God will guard your hearts and minds in Christ Jesus. Philippians 4:7

Do not be anxious about anything, but in everything, by prayer and petition, with thanksgiving, present your requests to God.

And the peace of God will guard your hearts and minds in Christ Jesus. Philippians 4:6, 7

84 Permission to photocopy this handout granted for local church use. Copyright © Cook Communications Ministries. Printed in Pick Up 'n' Do Lessons on Let's Hear It for the Fruit of the Spirit!

Have kids write or draw things that make them anxious inside the rainbow figure, then glue the rainbow closed. If you wish, let kids share what they wrote.

Let's pray together and officially give God all these worrisome things we've just written down. Have kids hold the prayer rainbows in their hands. **Dear Lord, when fearful things happen, our hearts get so full of worry that there's no room for anything else. We've written down the things that make us anxious, and now we give them to you. Please take our fears and fill our hearts with the sweet peace that can only come from you. We thank you and bless your name, Jesus, amen.**

Peace to You!

God invites us to unload all our fears and anxious thoughts on him. Cut out the rainbow figure, fold it at the middle and fold the flaps forward to make it stand up. On the inside, write down the fearful thoughts you'd like God to take from you. Then glue it closed and ask God to fill your heart with his peace.

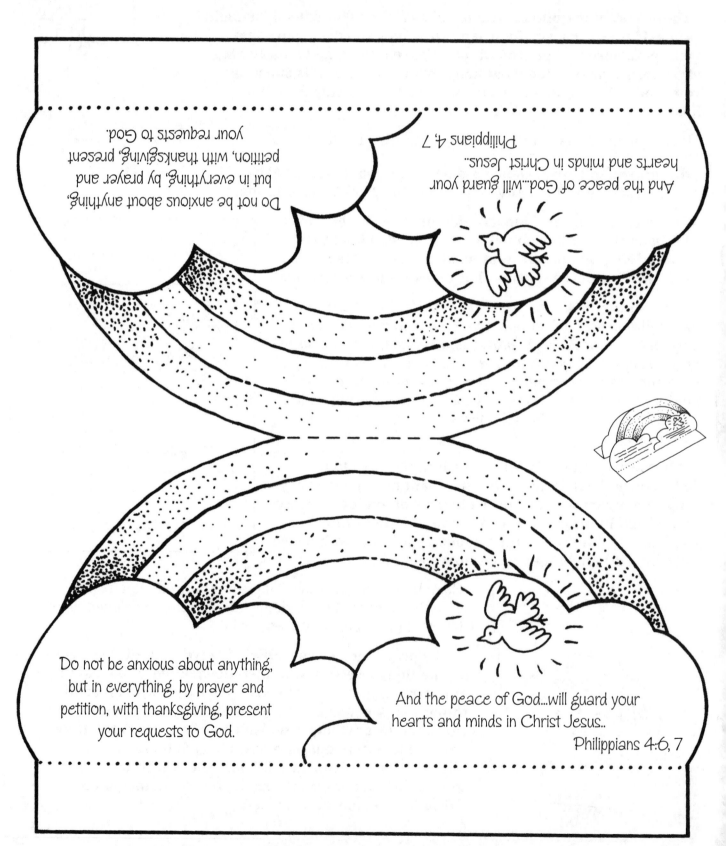

Do not be anxious about anything, but in everything, by prayer and petition, with thanksgiving, present your requests to God.

And the peace of God...will guard your hearts and minds in Christ Jesus..
Philippians 4:6, 7

Workshop Wonders

In today's Bible story we learned that Peter was in trouble—big trouble! King Herod imprisoned him for telling people about Jesus, and his friends were afraid he would be put to death. There was only one thing they could do—pray. And that's what they did.

■ **Share a time when you prayed for God to help someone you loved. What happened?**

As Peter's friends prayed, a God thing happened. Peter awoke to see a light in his prison cell. An angel of the Lord, one of God's messengers, had come to free him from the chains, the soldiers near him and the sentries who stood guard.

■ **What do you think Peter's first reaction was when the angel struck him?**

God knew all about Peter's problem and he sent help in the form of an angel. When we're in a tough spot and filled with worry, we never know what God will do to help us. But it's delicious to think about!

Set out pretzel sticks, gumdrops (or mini-marshmallows) and large marshmallows. Be sure you have plenty so kids can munch as they create. Finally, have each child take a paper plate. **Use this yummy stuff to make a scene or a character from today's Bible story. You might want build a Christian praying, or the angel God sent to set Peter free. Make a Roman guard, the cell where Peter was a prisoner, or one of the gates that opened all by itself.**

Circulate among kids as they work and invite them to tell you about what they're making. You may want to have the group plan figures that tell the story sequentially.

■ **What's your favorite part of this story? Why do you like that part?**

■ **What's one thing you're going to remember from this story?**

Let kids decide if they want to gobble their creations or take them to share with their families. Provide coffee filters or plastic bags for kids to transport their food sculptures.

Here are some last-minute instructions for this week! Repeat today's comforting Bible verse before kids leave.

"Do not be anxious about anything, but in everything, by prayer and petition, with thanksgiving, present your requests to God. And the peace of God, which transcends all understanding, will guard your hearts and your minds in Christ Jesus."

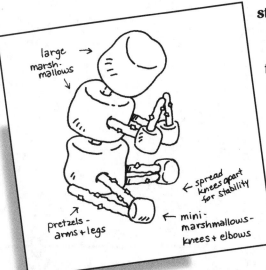

large marsh-mallows →

← spread apart knees apart for stability

pretzels - arms + legs

← mini-marshmallows - knees + elbows

Fold down the corners to start your paper airplane.

SPECIAL DELIVERY

TO

Be at peace.

Today at church we learned how an angel set Peter free from prison.

How did the Holy Spirit work in today's prison escape story?

Name the one thing that Peter's friends could do for him while he was in prison. (Pray). How do prayer and peace go together?

Be at peace and trust God! On a nice weather day use chalk to draw a nine-box hopscotch board on a sidewalk or driveway. Fill the boxes with the fruit of the Spirit using words or pictures. As you work, discuss with your friends how peace, love, joy, patience, kindness, goodness, faithfulness, gentleness and self-control all connect us to God. Play a round of hopscotch and collect the fruit of the Spirit from the board!

Bible Verse

"Do not be anxious about anything, but in everything, by prayer and petition, with thanksgiving, present your requests to God. And the peace of God, which transcends all understanding, will guard your hearts and your minds in Christ Jesus." Philippians 4:6, 7

◊ What makes you feel peaceful inside?
◊ How can you feel peaceful even when super bad things happen?
◊ What kinds of things can we put around the house to remind us that God is in control?

☆ Family FUN ☆

Live It! ☆

Crowd Control

Option

Get Set
LARGE GROUP ■ Greet kids and do a puppet skit. Schooner tells about moments he was glad to receive lots of attention.

❏ large bird puppet ❏ puppeteer

1

Bible 4U! Instant Drama
LARGE GROUP ■ Two dogs roam the streets of Lystra and discuss the amazing events that occurred during the visit of Paul and Barnabas.

❏ 2 actors ❏ copies of pp. 90-91, Dog Days in Lystra script ❏ 4 numbered balls
Optional: ❏ dog costumes ❏ Bibletime street set

2

Shepherd's Spot
SMALL GROUP ■ Use the "In the Zone" handout to help kids target times when it's challenging to practice self-control.

❏ Bibles ❏ pencils ❏ scissors ❏ copies of p. 94, In the Zone ❏ copies of p. 96, Special Delivery

Option

Workshop Wonders
SMALL GROUP ■ Create vignettes from today's story, then practice the fine art of self-control by not moving when a gentle feather tickles.

❏ Bible ❏ old plastic bowl ❏ colored water ❏ jar ❏ tack or nail ❏ large, soft feather

Bible Basis
People try to worship Paul.
Acts 14:8–18

Learn It!
The Holy Spirit helps us bring honor to God.

Live It!
Practice self-control.

Bible Verse
Humble yourselves before the Lord, and he will lift you up.
James 4:10

Quick Takes

Acts 14:8–18

14:8 In Lystra there sat a man crippled in his feet, who was lame from birth and had never walked.
9 He listened to Paul as he was speaking. Paul looked directly at him, saw that he had faith to be healed
10 and called out, "Stand up on your feet!" At that, the man jumped up and began to walk.
11 When the crowd saw what Paul had done, they shouted in the Lycaonian language, "The gods have come down to us in human form!"
12 Barnabas they called Zeus, and Paul they called Hermes because he was the chief speaker.
13 The priest of Zeus, whose temple was just outside the city, brought bulls and wreaths to the city gates because he and the crowd wanted to offer sacrifices to them.

14 But when the apostles Barnabas and Paul heard of this, they tore their clothes and rushed out into the crowd, shouting:
15 "Men, why are you doing this? We too are only men, human like you. We are bringing you good news, telling you to turn from these worthless things to the living God, who made heaven and earth and sea and everything in them.
16 In the past, he let all nations go their own way.
17 Yet he has not left himself without testimony: He has shown kindness by giving you rain from heaven and crops in their seasons; he provides you with plenty of food and fills your hearts with joy."
18 Even with these words, they had difficulty keeping the crowd from sacrificing to them.

Insights

For Paul and Barnabas, Lystra was just another town, another effective opportunity to tell about Jesus do and a miracle or two. Everyday stuff for these dynamic evangelists. But definitely not everyday stuff for the people of Lystra. So impressed were the townspeople by Barnabas and Paul that they proclaimed them to be the Greek gods Zeus and Hermes. They equated Barnabas with Zeus, the king of the Greek gods, and Paul with Hermes, the messenger of the Greek gods. We know Paul was the main spokesperson and preacher, which is probably why the locals thought him to be the messenger god.

Paul and Barnabas were appalled. They pleaded with the people to recognize them as mere men, servants of the living God. It never occurred to them to cash in on the benefits of instant celebrity.

How many people do you know who would refuse to be honored, served and presented with rich gifts? Paul and Barnabas could have selfishly milked their sudden popularity. But because their lives were controlled by God's Holy Spirit, they rejected the homage and passionately protested with the truth.

Who doesn't long for the limelight from time to time? Kids certainly do! Their eager young spirits long to be praised for growing accomplishments. Use this lesson to teach kids that self-control is a greater gift than popularity—a fruit of the Spirit that will serve them in all the ups and downs of life.

Get Set

Open with lively music, then greet the kids. **Today we'll learn that the Holy Spirit helps us bring honor to God. That means being humble and self-controlled. Schooner, I have a question for you.** *Schooner pops up.*

Leader: I have a question for you, Schooner.

Schooner: Shoot, boss.

Leader: What was one of your proudest moments?

Schooner: Let me think. I got it—hatching!

Leader: Hatching.

Schooner: If you're not impressed, you clearly don't understand. Peck-peck-pecking all scrunched up like that. Getting out of your shell is a tough job.

Leader: Hatching isn't quite the kind of thing I have in mind. I'm thinking of a time when you got applause and some 'atta boys for doing something terrific.

Schooner: I know! I know! The first time I climbed the monkey bars!

Leader: Parrots climb monkey bars?

Schooner: Yep. By using our most formidable asset.

Leader: Which is?

Schooner: Beaks! Parrots use their beaks to climb. It's like having an extra foot.

Leader: Ah. So you're a three-footed parrot?

Schooner: *Puh-leeze.*

Leader: What happened when you got to the top of the monkey bars?

Schooner: My friends and family circled overhead and squawked and talked and flapped their wings in applause.

Leader: *Schweet.*

Schooner: It was sweet. Then there was the time I did a triple loop into a roll into a hammerhead stall.

Leader: A hammerhead who?

Schooner: A hammerhead stall, boss. It's fancy flying. I go straight up as far as I can, then turn my nose down and spin down toward the ground. Just before my beak bites the dust, I pull up and fly away.

Leader: That would get some attention.

Schooner: No kidding. I almost got grounded by the P.A.A. I had to disappear for a little while.

Leader: And the P.A.A. would be…

Schooner: The Parrot Aviation Agency. You don't want to get in trouble with them.

Leader: I'll try to remember that. You know, a very similar thing happened to Paul and Barnabas.

Schooner: *(shocked)* They got grounded?

Leader: No, but they got a little more attention than they wanted.

Schooner: What kind of trick did they do?

Leader: No trick at all. Paul did a miracle. He healed a man who had never been able to walk.

Schooner: And they got in trouble for that?

Leader: Not the kind of trouble you're used to getting into.

Schooner: What other kind of trouble is there?

Leader: Being so popular that people went bonkers and said they were gods.

Schooner: Whoa—how cool would that be? People would give you presents, wait on you hand and foot, do whatever you said…

Leader: Which is precisely why it took a lot of self-control to stop the crowds from treating them like that.

Schooner: You mean they missed their chance to be completely adored?

Leader: Yep. On purpose. They knew only God should get that kind of attention.

Schooner: I guess I have a lot to learn, don't I, boss?

Leader: Then let's get to it.

Schooner: *Squawk!* Bible 4U! straight ahead!

1 Bible 4U!

Paul and Barnabas are on the go, as always, traveling from town to town to spread the Good News about Jesus. And this was no pleasure cruise, believe me! When they got to a new town, Paul and Barnabas would find the synagogue and start preaching there. Many people would put their faith in Jesus. The others would get mad and chase Paul and Barnabas out of town. So Paul and Barnabas got to be experts at fast getaways. That's what happened when Paul and Barnabas visited Iconium.

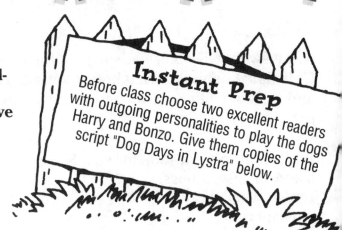

Instant Prep

Before class choose two excellent readers with outgoing personalities to play the dogs Harry and Bonzo. Give them copies of the script "Dog Days in Lystra" below.

for Overachievers

Have a two-person drama team prepare the story. Dress the actors in dog costumes. Prepare a set that looks like a Bibletime street scene.

Crowds of people believed in Jesus. The people who didn't believe got as many people mad at Paul and Barnabas as they could. When the angry crowd came after Paul and Barnabas, they scooted out of town. Next stop: the sleepy little town of Lystra. You would think Paul and Barnabas would have been ready for a little break, but not those two! They immediately began telling everyone about the living God. And they healed a man who couldn't walk.

And the results? Well, you'll just have to see what happened.

Dog Days in Lystra
Based on Acts 14:8–18

Harry: Hey, Bonzo!

Bonzo: It's my old buddy Harry. What's an old dog like you doing in a place like this?

Harry: Checking out all the goodies in the street.

Bonzo: Goodies in the street? I didn't think this was garbage day.

Harry: It's not. It's a whole lot better than garbage day.

Bonzo: So has the town of Lystra started a "Be Kind to Dogs' Day" or what?

Harry: It's more like a "Be Kind to gods' Day."

Bonzo: Okay, now I'm really confused.

Harry: You know how the folks around here believe in Greek gods?

Bonzo: Yeah—it's so silly. They make these stone statues and worship them and bring them offerings. That temple to the god Zeus is the nicest building in town.

Harry: Well, for a few moments today the town folks thought that two gods had come to visit us as people.

Bonzo: You're kidding! They must have been really messed up! Everyone knows that those Greek gods are fake. They don't walk and talk. They're just big lumps of stone that sit in the temples.

Harry: I know that and you know that, but sometimes people aren't as smart as dogs.

Bonzo: *Rrrruff!* So what made people think these gods had come? And didn't you say something about a treat in the street?

Harry: Slow down there, ole' buddy. One question at a time.

Bonzo: Okay. Let's start with the treats. Walk with me.

They walk around sniffing.

Harry: Would you check that out? That's some of the tastiest meat I've ever seen.

Bonzo: Just sitting here waiting to be snarfed.

Harry: You feeling hungry?

They both pounce on the meat and pretend to feed, then sit down and lick their paws.

Bonzo: How good was that? Steak Tartare.

Harry: Do you think it could have used a little mustard?

Bonzo: No, no, no! I prefer A1 Sauce®.

Harry: Whatever makes you drool…

They lick their paws then rub their faces.

Bonzo: Now that our tummies are full, how about the rest of the story? What was this prime rib doing in the street? Does it have anything to do with the people who were supposed to be gods?

Harry: It has everything to do with them. See, these two men named Paul and Barnabas came to town preaching about Jesus.

Bonzo: Who's Jesus?

Harry: The son of the living God!

Bonzo: The real living God—not one of these fake idols they have in the temples around here?

Harry: The real living God. I hung around an alley and heard what Paul and Barnabas had to say. God sent Jesus to be the Savior of the world. He told people that God loves them. People who believe in him are called Christians. They keep spreading the Good News about Jesus.

Bonzo: Are these Christians good guys?

Harry: You bet they are! You know that man who used to hang around here begging?

Bonzo: The one who couldn't walk?

Harry: That one. He believed what Paul and Barnabas were saying. Paul told him, "Stand up on your feet." The next thing I knew, he was walking!

Bonzo: But he's never been able to walk.

Harry: Precisely. It was a miracle! That's why everyone thought Paul and Barnabas were gods. The priest from the temple of Zeus brought them bulls and wreaths so the people could worship them.

Bonzo: That's where the prime rib came from?

Harry: Yep.

Bonzo: Paul and Barnabas must have loved being treated like gods!

Harry: As a matter of fact, they didn't. They rushed out into the crowd and told people to stop worshiping them. They said, "We're human, just like you."

Bonzo: Well, I'll be a fuzzy fleabag. Almost anybody I know would like getting that kind of special treatment.

Harry: Not these guys. They were all about getting the people to praise God.

Bonzo: How could they have that kind of self-control? Doesn't everyone want to be powerful and get lots of attention?

Harry: They love God. That's what makes them different.

Bonzo: So it's more important to them to love God than to be rich and famous?

Harry: Yep.

Bonzo: Wow. The God of Paul and Barnabas must be able to change people's hearts. You won't find any of the fake stone gods around here doing that.

Harry: That's right. Just ask the man who got healed today.

Bonzo: *(pauses to sniff)* I was sure I caught a whiff of fresh meat. Do you think there might be more treats in the streets?

Harry: *(sniffs)* Oh yeah, baby.

Bonzo: We're outta here!

They exit sniffing.

Paul and Barnabas passed up an opportunity for instant fame and glory. Let's see if you know why, when these men could have been honored as gods, they urged people to praise the one and only living God.

Toss the four numbered balls to different parts of the room. Bring kids with the balls to the front one-by-one and ask these questions. Allow kids to get help from the group if they need it. After each correct answer, let kids drop their balls into a bag.

 ■ Why did the people of Lystra think Paul and Barnabas were gods?

 ■ If you had been there that day, what would you say to people who had seen the miraculous healing and thought Paul and Barnabas were gods?

 ■ How could Paul and Barnabas have enough self-control to push away the praise and gifts they could have received?

 ■ Who are the most popular, famous people you can think of? Do they give credit to God, or keep all the praise for themselves?

Did you ever watch a game show on TV when someone won a lot a money? When Paul healed the lame man in Lystra, it was like hitting the jackpot. Gifts and honors and praises came from all sides. People would have done anything they asked. Boy, if I were in that situation I might be tempted to take the crowd up on their offer. "Bring it on—I'll take whatever you want to give me." It takes a ton of self-control to say, "No, this isn't about me. It's about God. I'm just an ordinary guy like all of you."

Self-control is a fruit of the spirit. It's God working in us that gives us the self-control not to brag and take credit for the good things God does. Self-control helps us rein in lots of other things that are wrong too, like being crabby, mouthing off or doing what we feel like doing instead of what we know is right.

Bible Verse
Humble yourselves before the Lord, and he will lift you up.
James 4:10

 The Holy Spirit whispers in our hearts and reminds us to do what honors God— not what we feel like doing at the moment. Today in your small groups you'll discover what a positive difference self-control can make in your life.

Dismiss kids to their shepherd groups.

2 Shepherd's Spot

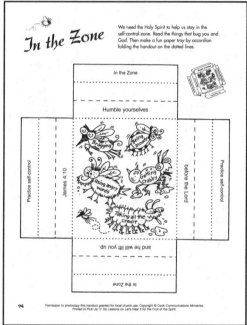

Gather your small group and help kids find Acts 14 in their Bibles.

We've had lots of stories where people get in trouble for preaching about Jesus and doing miracles in his name. This one is a switch—the folks in Lystra wanted to *worship* Paul and Barnabas. Let's see what Paul and Barnabas did for crowd control.

Have volunteers take turns reading Acts 14:8–18 aloud.

■ **Suppose Paul and Barnabas hadn't used self-control and instructed the people to worship God. What might have happened?**

Self-control means making a wise, God-honoring choice when you might be tempted to do what feels good at the moment. You might say it helps you box up actions that aren't pleasing to God. Pass out the "In the Zone" handout. Have kids cut it out on the solid lines, then fold up on the dotted lines and down on the dashed lines to form a tray with stand-up sides.

Practicing self-control means something different for each of us. For instance, I might be in the habit of bragging, but bragging might not be a problem for you at all. Maybe I never get moody or talk back, but that might be a big problem for some of you. We all have our weak points. The cool thing is, God made us and he knows exactly how to help us. How do we ask for God's help? That's easy!

Ask a volunteer to read James 4:10: *"Humble yourselves before the Lord, and he will lift you up."*

■ **If you had a problem with bragging, what might your prayer sound like when you ask** for God's help? How about a prayer to control angry words—what would that sound like?

In the center of your zone, you'll see lots of different things that can be self-control issues. Take a moment to put a little "x" by each thing that can be a problem for you. You may want to ask kids to share their self-control issues.

Close with prayer. **Heavenly father, you're great and almighty. Everything we are and everything we have comes from you. You know our strengths and our weaknesses. I pray for** (mention each child by name). **When we're tempted to act selfishly, help us use the self-control only your Spirit can give. We want to honor you with our lives more than anything. Amen.**

In the Zone

We need the Holy Spirit to help us stay in the self-control zone. Read the things that bug you and God. Then make a fun paper tray by accordion folding the handout on the dotted lines.

In the Zone

Humble yourselves

Practice self-control

James 4:10

Using angry words

Bragging

Being moody

Getting Crabby

Taking all the credit

before the Lord

Practice self-control

and he will lift you up.

In the Zone

Use this simple experiment to start your workshop time. **Time is on our side when we practice self-control. Let's prove it!** Use a tack to prick a hole in the bottom of a plastic bowl. Set the bowl on top of a jar. Pour in colored water. Watch as the water drips to slowly fill the jar. **Tick. *Drip.* Tock. *Drip.* We'll check our water clock later to see how much water—I mean, time!—we spend practicing self-control.**

> ### Get List:
> - ❑ Bible
> - ❑ old plastic bowl
> - ❑ colored water
> - ❑ jar
> - ❑ tack or nail
> - ❑ soft feather

Paul and Barnabas would never forget their trip to Lystra. Something very unexpected happened to them there, and they had to decide quickly how they would respond.

Separate your class into groups. **Let's be sure we have the picture of this story in our minds. In your group, choose someone for each of the roles in this story: crippled man, Paul, Barnabas, priest of Zeus and the crowd.** If you have large groups, suggest that some kids could also play inanimate roles, such as the city gates and the bull the priest brought to sacrifice.

Everybody got your role? Now let's put the picture together. Have someone read Acts 14:8–14. **Arrange yourselves so that you are dramatizing this scene. What would the crippled man be doing? What would the crowd be doing? How about the priest? Paul and Barnabas? Act out your scene for just a minute. Then when I shout "Freeze," stay in whatever position you are in at that moment.**

Allow the kids to begin their dramas, then quickly call out "Freeze." Take out your feather and wave it around a little bit. **I'm going to come around with my feather. I might tickle your chin, or your nose, or drag it softly down your arm. Your job is to stay still! The feather might make you want to laugh, so self-control is going to be really important. If you laugh or move, you have to sit down. Ready?**

Go around the room and tease kids with the feather. Be sure keep the feather touch brief and avoid any inappropriate contact. You may have some who giggle when they see others giggling—be sure to have them sit down as well. After you've visited each group, gather kids in a group.

■ **How was resisting the feather like what Paul and Barnabas had to do?** *(Kids had to use self-control to resist the feather. Paul and Barnabas had to use self-control to resist being worshiped.)*

■ **How did Paul and Barnabas honor God with their self-control?** *(They told the people why they should worship the true God.)*

Before kids leave, say, **Time to check the clock!** Walk over to the water-clock experiment. Mark the height of the water. **Your parents will be very proud to know all the time you spent practicing self-control!** You may wish to leave the clock "ticking" throughout the day for kids to check on.

Fold down the corners to start your paper airplane.

SPECIAL DELIVERY

TO

Practice self-control.

Today at church we learned that the Holy Spirit helps us bring honor to God. Share with your parents what the Paul did in today's Bible story that caused the crowd to want to crown him god. (Paul healed a crippled man.)

Family FUN

Let's find a fun way to practice self-control. Find a joke book at home. Then gather your family and take turns telling jokes. Make faces as you go! But be sure to tell everyone up front that the object of the game is to practice self-control. Absolutely, positively no laughing! He, who laughs first, laughs last—and exits the game.

Bible Verse

Humble yourselves before the Lord, and he will lift you up.
James 4:10

Live It!

◇ If you were in a tempting situation, what would your prayer for self-control sound like?

◇ If you could design a T-shirt of today's story, what would it say? What would it look like?

◇ Read the Bible Verse, James 4:10 aloud. How does believing the message of this verse help you practice self-control?

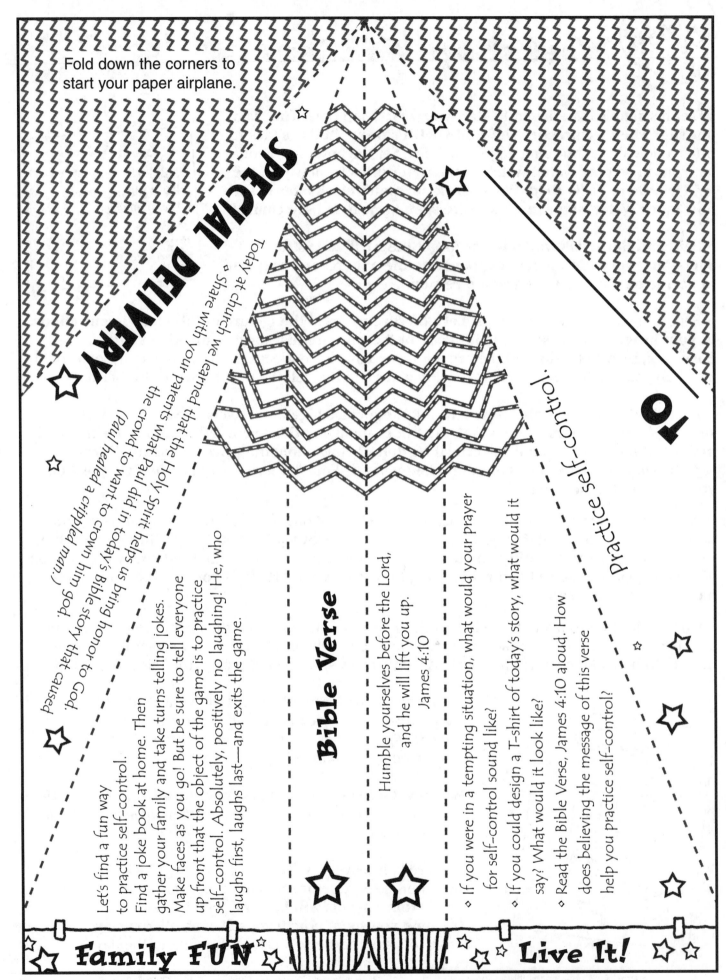

Home Away from Home

Option

Get Set
LARGE GROUP ■ Greet kids and do a puppet skit. Schooner learns that a small kindness can make a big difference.

❑ large bird puppet ❑ puppeteer

1

Bible 4U! Instant Drama
LARGE GROUP ■ Lydia's housemaid tells a friend about the new friends who are staying at Lydia's house.

❑ 2 actors ❑ copies of pp. 100-101, The Maid's Tale script ❑ 4 numbered balls
Optional: ❑ Bibletime costumes ❑ vegetable cart ❑ shopping baskets

2

Shepherd's Spot
SMALL GROUP ■ Use the "Top Secret" handout to help kids make secret plans to show kindness.

❑ Bibles ❑ pencils ❑ scissors ❑ copies of p. 104, Top Secret ❑ copies of p. 106, Special Delivery

Option

Workshop Wonders
SMALL GROUP ■ Make a treat with eye and taste appeal and learn how to treat guests with kindness.

❑ square cloth or paper napkins ❑ plastic spoons ❑ clear plastic cups
❑ chocolate and vanilla instant pudding mix ❑ milk ❑ mixing bowls, spoons or whisks ❑ aerosol whipped cream ❑ sprinkles

Bible Basis
Lydia believes and shows kindness to Paul. Acts 16:11–15

Learn It!
God's people show kindness.

Live It!
Be kind.

Bible Verse
Whoever is kind to the needy honors God.
Proverbs 14:31

Quick Takes

Acts 16:11–15

16:11 From Troas we put out to sea and sailed straight for Samothrace, and the next day on to Neapolis.
12 From there we traveled to Philippi, a Roman colony and the leading city of that district of Macedonia. And we stayed there several days.
13 On the Sabbath we went outside the city gate to the river, where we expected to find a place of prayer. We sat down and began to speak to the women who had gathered there.

14 One of those listening was a woman named Lydia, a dealer in purple cloth from the city of Thyatira, who was a worshiper of God. The Lord opened her heart to respond to Paul's message.
15 When she and the members of her household were baptized, she invited us to her home. "If you consider me a believer in the Lord," she said, "come and stay at my house." And she persuaded us.

Insights

This account of Paul's encounter with Lydia gives us brief but fascinating insights into the life of a woman who played a key role in the birth and growth of the church at Philippi. The text calls her "a worshiper of God" which may indicate that she was a Gentile who admired Judaism and participated in its practices as an outsider. Being a dealer in purple cloth did not necessarily make Lydia a wealthy woman as many have speculated. She could have been involved in the dyeing of the cloth, not just the trading of it. Cloth dyeing was difficult, dirty work. If Lydia managed such an operation, she could have been a hardworking woman of modest means who prevailed on the traveling missionaries to share her home, which may also have been her place of work.

Whatever Lydia's financial circumstances, she will always be characterized by a heart open to God, given to kindness and hospitality. After hearing Paul's message, she and the members of the household were baptized. It's likely that the church that grew in Philippi met in Lydia's home. Much later, in his letter to the Philippians, Paul recalled, "Moreover, as you Philippians know, in the early days of your acquaintance with the gospel, when I set out from Macedonia, not one church shared with me in the matter of giving and receiving, except you only; for even when I was in Thessalonica, you sent me aid again and again when I was in need" (Philippians 4:15, 16). What a marvelous legacy Lydia left to all of us!

Kids, who live essentially in the moment, have little idea of the far-reaching power of a kindness shared. Use this lesson to show them that God can multiply their simple acts of kindness into great things for his kingdom.

Open with lively music, then greet the kids. **There's an old saying that goes: You can catch more bees with honey than with vinegar. In other words, kindness works. Bee kind! Schooner, come on up here. I have another old saying that I'd like to share with you.** *Schooner pops up.*

Schooner: Share away!

Leader: The saying starts…

Schooner: Wait a minute, boss, you mean old saying, don't you?

Leader: Old saying?

Schooner: Is the saying old or is it new?

Leader: Old or new doesn't matter, Schooner. It's a good saying.

Schooner: All righty then. Because you did say old at first.

Leader: *(shakes head)* Sometimes you make mountains out of molehills, birdie.

Schooner: Is that another saying, boss?

Leader: Yes, it is.

Schooner: Is it old?

Leader: I'm the one that's getting old here. Now, where was I?

Schooner: A saying, boss.

Leader: Yes. Here it is: Good things come in small packages.

Schooner: Hey, that's me!

Leader: You?

Schooner: Me!

Leader: You are a small package, Schooner.

Schooner: Small but sassy. *Squawk!*

Leader: You're one of a kind.

Schooner: *(lays his head on Leader's shoulder)* Thank you.

Leader: Speaking of kind—you just hit on our topic for today.

Schooner: I did?

Leader: Yep. We're going to talk about being kind. And how the smallest kindness can mean the world to someone in need.

Schooner: Like a kind word?

Leader: Very good. A kind word is not a big thing. But it can sure make someone's day!

Schooner: *(lifts beak)* Let's see…

Leader: Can you come up with something else?

Schooner: Kind hugs?

Leader: Also good!

Schooner: Kind rugs, kind bugs, kind slugs…

Leader: You're getting carried away, Schooner.

Schooner: Sorry, boss.

Leader: In today's Bible story we hear of a woman who offers her home to Paul and some of his traveling buddies.

Schooner: Was that a big or a small kindness?

Leader: What do you think?

Schooner: Don't know, boss.

Leader: To some people that might be a big kindness.

Schooner: And to others just an everyday kind of kindness.

Leader: All in all, what matters is that Jesus wants us to be kind to one another. We have no idea how God can grow a small kindness into something great for his kingdom.

Schooner: Paul must have liked being invited to someone's house. There's nothing like the comfort of a good nest!

Leader: Like melted butter on popcorn, kindness really hits the spot!

Schooner: Kindness is like popcorn?

Leader: I was just saying that it hits the spot.

Schooner: Are you trying to confuse me, boss?

Leader: *(shakes head)* How's about going straight to the Bible story? I'm sure that will make everything perfectly clear.

Schooner: Sounds like a plan.

Leader: You like dogs, don't you?

Schooner: Sure I do. What does that have to do with the Bible story?

Leader: You'll see in just a minute. In Bible 4U! we'll hear the story from a dog's point of view.

Schooner: Sounds like dog days in Bible 4U! up next!

1 Bible 4U!

Welcome to Bible 4U! Theatre. Grab your seat by one of the open-air markets in the bustling city of Philippi. Philippi is a Roman colony and a leading city in Macedonia. Imagine the hustle and bustle of street vendors and shoppers mixed with the sounds of children running about and Roman soldiers watching over everything. It's a noisy place with lambs bleating, birds squawking and roosters crowing from their pens in the marketplace. The smell of fish brought to the market from the nearby port at Neopolis mixes in the air with the smell of fruits and vegetables and the not-so-fresh smell of the animals!

We're just in time to overhear a couple of women talking about the very beginning of the Christian church in the continent of Europe! We'll hear how Paul and Silas along with Dr. Luke and young Timothy preached to a group of women at a prayer meeting on the riverbank.

Let's listen in on our two shoppers conversation and hear how the kindness of one woman watered the seed of Christianity for an entire continent!

The Maid's Tale
Based on Acts 16:11-15

Josie: *Yoo-hoo* Ruthie! It's me, Josie. Am I glad I ran into you!

Ruth: *(smiling)* Why hello there, Miss Josie. What's new?

Josie: *(bustling about)* I had to come to the market to buy MORE food for Lydia. We have guests, you know, and it seems I'm cooking all the time! But I'm not complaining.

Ruth: I didn't know Lydia had guests. But then I'm not surprised. She's always helping people whenever she has the chance.

Josie: *(talking excitedly)* You didn't know about our guests? Oh my goodness, have I got a lot to tell you! So many things have happened this week. I didn't realize I hadn't seen you since all the excitement. I don't even know where to start!

Ruth: *(calmly patting Josie)* Ok, Josie, slow down. Start at the beginning.

Josie: The beginning. Well, Lydia is just the very best boss. She's so kind to all her workers. And she's the brightest businesswoman I know. She's such an expert at making purple cloth. She knows all about crushing the shells of tiny sea creatures to make the purple dye and choosing the very best cloth for her customers. She's always fair and honest so people like to do business with her. It's just amazing to see that such a kind woman can hold her own in business and...

Ruth: (interrupting) I already know about Lydia's business, Josie. I want to hear about the new exciting things.

Josie: (taking a deep breath) Sorry I was being an airhead. Let's see…you know that Lydia is a worshiper of the One True God and that she meets with other women down by the river to pray.

Ruth: Yes—down by the riverside.

Josie: Hey, do you think that would make a good song?

Ruth: Back to the story, Josie.

Josie: Right. So we were praying down by the riverside when four men interrupted our meeting.

Ruth: (looking concerned) Oh— I hope they weren't there to make trouble!

Josie: No, no, nothing like that! There were two rabbis, a doctor and a younger man.

Ruth: (frustrated) I think I've heard this joke…

Josie: (looking serious) This is no joke! Paul, Silas, Dr. Luke and young Timothy came to the prayer meeting and began to tell about Jesus.

Ruth: Jesus…isn't he the man that created such a stir down in Jerusalem?

Josie: Yes ma'am! But he was not just a man! Paul told us how Jesus was the one and only Son of God!

Ruth: Son of God? How can that be?

Josie: Paul told us that God sent his Son to earth to show us God's love and that Jesus paid the price for our sins when he died on the cross. Then he rose again and sent the Holy Spirit to help those who believe in him.

Ruth: You mean Jesus is the promised Messiah?

Josie: Yes, yes! The Holy Spirit opened Lydia's heart and she believed in Jesus. Then all the members of our household, including me, (chest swells with pride) were baptized right there in the river!

Ruth: (amazed) Baptized! Just like that?

Josie: Just like that. Just think, Ruth—I have a savior! And a houseful of company! Lydia invited Paul, Silas, Dr. Luke and Timothy into her home. She said they could stay as long as they were in Philippi. We're taking care of them so they can spend all their time telling people about Jesus.

Ruth: That's so kind of Lydia.

Josie: It feels so wonderful for all of us to be part of something really big and important!

Ruth: What do you mean?

Josie: Well, Paul and his team of missionaries have traveled through Judea, Syria and Galatia telling people about Jesus. And then they crossed the Aegean Sea to come to our city. Philippi is the first city on this whole continent to hear about Jesus! Lydia was the first one to believe, and now we have a group of Christians meeting at our house.

Ruth: Wow. I'd like to be part of something like that.

Josie: Then come! We'd be thrilled to have you. Wait 'til you hear Paul speak. There's a meeting tonight.

Ruth: I'll be there!

Josie: Then I'll grab a couple more veggies for the stew.

Ruth: That's kind of you, Josie.

Josie: It's the least I can do. I see everything so differently now. I'm not just a servant— I'm serving the living God! And what we're doing—taking care of Paul and his friends— is going to make a difference in our town. Maybe even in the whole world!

Ruth: I can't wait to hear more about this!

Josie: See you tonight, then. Be sure to bring a good appetite.

Ruth: I'd never come without my appetite! Bye!

They exit.

kay, all you lovely people, what kind of fruit did you pick up during our shopping trip? Did you pick up the figs or maybe the apples? Or did you find the fruit of the Spirit that Ms. Lydia had a lot of? You know the kind of fruit I mean—the fruit of kindness!

Toss the four numbered balls to different parts of the room. Bring the kids with the balls to the front one-by-one and ask these questions. Allow kids to get help from the group if they need it. After each correct answer, let kids drop their balls into a bag.

 ■ How did Lydia's kindness help the work of the four missionaries?

■ What do you think made Lydia decide to be kind to Paul and his friends?

 ■ After all of Paul's scary adventures, what do you think it was like to be welcomed to a home away from home?

 ■ How can kindness draw people to God?

Radical kindness—going above and beyond what is expected—that's part of the fruit the Holy Spirit wants to grow in each of us. Lydia was a busy, successful businesswoman who probably had a million things on her to do list. No one would have blamed her if she'd decided not to take time for company—especially guests who might stay for a while. But Lydia made the kind choice. God gave her a tender heart for the needs of others.

When Lydia opened her home to Paul and his friends, she could hardly have imagined the difference it would make. The church Paul started there grew and shared with Christians in other countries. Later in his life, Paul wrote a letter to that church. You can read it in your Bible today—it's the book of Philippians.

Bible Verse
Whoever is kind to the needy honors God.
Proverbs 14:31

An act of kindness, big or small, can make a big difference in God's kingdom. Kindness Rules! Today in your small groups you'll get to plan some acts of kindness of your own. Who knows how God will use what you plan today!

Dismiss kids to their shepherd groups.

② Shepherd's Spot

Gather your small group and help kids find Acts 16 in their Bibles.

Sometimes a little kindness does more good than we can imagine. Today's Bible story is an example of how one woman's kindness helped spread the Good News about Jesus to places it had never been heard.

Have volunteers take turns reading Acts 16:11–15 aloud.

■ **What kind of extra work does it create to have several guests in your home?**

■ **Why do you think Lydia was willing to take on that extra work?**

Kindness comes in all shapes and sizes. Sometimes it's as simple as an encouraging word like, "Good job in class today." Sometimes it takes time and planning, like Lydia's hospitality. One thing that's really fun is to plan a secret kindness mission for a friend or family member.

Pass out the "Top Secret" handout. Ask a volunteer to read Proverbs 14:31 aloud: *"Whoever is kind to the needy honors God."* **The Holy Spirit helps us realize what the people around us need. Lydia realized that Paul and his friends needed a place to stay. Think for a moment about your friends and family members. What kinds of needs do they have? What secret acts of kindness could you plan?**

Give kids a moment to brainstorm and write their ideas. Invite volunteers to share some of their plans. Show kids how to cut out the "Top Secret" booklet, fold it and tuck the right side into the fold on the left side.

I think there are going to be some happy people in your lives when you carry out your plans! Let's pray that God will use our acts of kindness in wonderful ways.

Invite kids to share prayer concerns, then close with prayer. **Dear Heavenly Father, we thank you for the kind people you've brought into our lives—people who see our needs. We ask you to make us aware of the needs of the people around us. Today we bring before you (mention kids' concerns). Help us carry out our plans for kindness in a way that will bring honor to you. In Jesus' name, amen.**

TOP SECRET

There's nothing more fun than carrying out a secret kindness mission without being caught! Plan four kindness missions in the booklet—then fold it closed and carry on!

In my neighborhood

Your choice

The plan:

Accomplish four secret acts of kindness without being caught. Whoever is kind to the needy honors God.
Proverbs 14:31

At school

TOP SECRET

Initial here:

At home

Workshop Wonders

Plan to invite special guests to your Workshop Wonder time today. You may choose to bring in a neighboring class or various church staff members. **Today we're going to whip up a little kindness for some guests. Our example for kindness in action is Lydia. She was a merchant who lived in the bustling city of Philippi. Her business was selling purple cloth, an expensive item worn by the rich.**

■ **Can you think of an expensive item in today's world that only a few can afford?**

Lydia and her friends were praying by the river when Paul found them and told them about Jesus. Lydia opened her heart and became a believer. In fact, she was baptized along with her household. Immediately, she insisted that Paul and his traveling companions stay at her house. Lydia's hospitality and kindness helped Paul focus on starting a church in Philippi.

Let's set the stage for some hospitality of our own by making a snack to share that looks as good as it tastes!

Let kids work in groups to whip up different flavors of instant pudding. Have them spoon the pudding in layers into plastic cups. Be sure to prepare enough so the kids can enjoy the treat as well. Let them top the pudding cups with a squirt of whipped cream and a few colorful sprinkles.

Now let's set a spiffy table with the pudding cups and fancy folded napkins. Hand out napkins and have kids follow you step by step through the napkin folding process.

1. Open the napkin and spread it out diamond-wise.
2. Bring the bottom point to the top, creating a triangle.
3. Fold the corners toward the center and tuck one corner inside the other.
4. Turn the folded napkin over. Fold the top point down.
5. Tuck a spoon into the pocket.

Before your guests arrive, talk with your kids about how you will make them feel welcome. Discuss topics for conversation. Stress the importance of learning and using each guest's name.

Encourage kids to think about when they might prepare this treat for their families as an act of kindness.

Get List:
- ☐ square cloth or paper napkins
- ☐ plastic spoons
- ☐ clear plastic cups
- ☐ chocolate and vanilla instant pudding mix
- ☐ milk
- ☐ mixing bowls, spoons or whisks
- ☐ aerosol whipped cream
- ☐ sprinkles

Fold down the corners to start your paper airplane.

SPECIAL DELIVERY

TO

God's people show kindness. Be kind.

Bible Verse

Whoever is kind to the needy honors God. Proverbs 14:31

Today at church we learned that a little kindness can make a big difference! Tell what Paul shared with Lydia. What did Lydia do for Paul? How did Lydia's kindness help build God's kingdom? How can we share with Paul?

Set out slips of paper, pencils and a small goldfish bowl or clear glass jar. Brainstorm and write down as many small acts of kindness as you can think of. Write each idea on three slips of paper and drop them into the bowl. When someone is down, go fishing for kindness! Take an idea from the bowl and do it. When you've been so kind to each other that your bowl is empty, add new ideas along with old favorites.

◊ Have you witnessed an act of kindness that you'll never forget?
◊ Who's the kindest person you've ever known?
◊ Read Proverbs 14:31 together. Do we know someone in need? How can we show kindness to that person?

☆ Family FUN ☆

Live It!

Jailhouse Rock

Get Set
LARGE GROUP ■ Greet kids and do a puppet skit. Schooner learns that there's a difference between happiness and godly joy.

❏ large bird puppet   ❏ puppeteer

Bible 4U! Instant Drama
LARGE GROUP ■ The jailer's children hear Paul and Silas singing in jail, then experience the earthquake and the joy of answered prayer.

❏ 3 actors   ❏ copies of pp. 110-111, Jailbreak script   ❏ 4 numbered balls
Optional: ❏ sets for street scene and Bibletime home   ❏ tunics and a soldier's costume

Shepherd's Spot
SMALL GROUP ■ Use the "Jumpin' for Joy" handout to make cards that will encourage friends to find God's joy in difficult situations.

❏ Bibles ❏ pencils ❏ scissors ❏ copies of p. 114, Jumpin for Joy ❏ copies of p. 116, Special Delivery

Workshop Wonders
SMALL GROUP ■ Make licorice and pretzel chains and talk about how Paul and Silas knew God's joy even when they were chained in prison.

❏ licorice ropes or ribbon   ❏ mini-pretzel twists

Bible Basis
Paul and Silas in prison. Acts 16:16–19, 23, 25–34

Learn It!
Joy comes from knowing God.

Live It!
Be joyful.

Bible Verse
Be joyful always; pray continually; give thanks in all circumstances.
1 Thessalonians 5:16–18

Quick Takes

Acts 16:16–19, 23, 25–34

16:16 Once when we were going to the place of prayer, we were met by a slave girl who had a spirit by which she predicted the future. She earned a great deal of money for her owners by fortune telling.

17 This girl followed Paul and the rest of us, shouting, "These men are servants of the Most High God, who are telling you the way to be saved."

18 She kept this up for many days. Finally Paul became so troubled that he turned round and said to the spirit, "In the name of Jesus Christ I command you to come out of her!" At that moment the spirit left her.

19 When the owners of the slave girl realized that their hope of making money was gone, they seized Paul and Silas and dragged them into the marketplace to face the authorities.

23 After they had been severely flogged, they were thrown into prison, and the jailer was commanded to guard them carefully.

25 About midnight Paul and Silas were praying and singing hymns to God, and the other prisoners were listening to them.

26 Suddenly there was such a violent earth-quake that the foundations of the prison were shaken. At once all the prison doors flew open, and everybody's chains came loose.

27 The jailer woke up, and when he saw the prison doors open, he drew his sword and was about to kill himself because he thought the prisoners had escaped.

28 But Paul shouted, "Don't harm yourself! We are all here!"

29 The jailer called for lights, rushed in and fell trembling before Paul and Silas.

30 He then brought them out and asked, "Sirs, what must I do to be saved?"

31 They replied, "Believe in the Lord Jesus, and you will be saved—you and your household." 32 Then they spoke the word of the Lord to him and to all the others in his house.

33 At that hour of the night the jailer took them and washed their wounds; then immediately he and all his family were baptized.

34 The jailer brought them into his house and set a meal before them; he was filled with joy because he had come to believe in God—he and his whole family.

Insights

No matter how you look at it, being locked away in a foul Roman prison was no cause for joy. Imagine the stench of unwashed people with inadequate toilet facilities, the language that bombarded the narrow hallways, the guards' brutality.

Before Paul and Silas were locked away in prison, they'd been chased by a mob and beaten. Bruised and bleeding, they were locked away in the most dismal part of the Philippian prison with their legs chained in stocks. With no one to tend their wounds except interested insects and vermin that crawled across the damp, filthy floor, the two missionaries might well have slipped into despair.

As their joyful hymn singing floated through the dismal prison, everyone must have wondered if Paul and Silas were out of their minds. What did they have to sing about? What was the source of this joy that sustained them in the worst possible circumstances?

The answer is simple: they knew God. They had served him faithfully and courageously in the face of violent opposition and they knew he was not oblivious to their plight. In the depths of a miserable prison, they knew the comfort of being in the palm of God's hand. Use this lesson to help kids understand that joy doesn't come from having everything turn out well—it comes from knowing that our lives are in the hands of our loving, mighty God.

Get Set

Open with lively music, then greet the kids. **It's wonderful to see you all here today. Today's we'll learn that joy comes from knowing God. And it's a great word—joy. I love it! Schooner, hop up here and let's get a little joy started!** *Schooner pops up.*

Leader: I can't think of a better word in all the world than joy!

Schooner: Well, I can think of a few.

Leader: For example?

Schooner: Food.

Leader: I see.

Schooner: Almonds.

Leader: *(repeats)* Almonds. That's a nice word.

Schooner: Smoked, roasted or straight from the shell, nuts make me happy.

Leader: Oh, the things I could say about you and nuts!

Schooner: *(continues)*…and fruit and juice.

Leader: I see.

Schooner: And raindrops on roses and whiskers on kittens.

Leader: I think that song's been done.

Schooner: These are a few of my happy things.

Leader: Wonderful, Schooner. But today we're talking about the word joy.

Schooner: That's what I'm talking about, boss. Happiness.

Leader: Joy is even better than happiness.

Schooner: Why's that, boss?

Leader: Because joy comes from knowing God.

Schooner: Oh. Joy is a God thing, huh?

Leader: Precisely.

Schooner: So…happiness is a dish of ice cream and joy is the hot fudge?

Leader: Well…

Schooner: Or happiness is chocolate cake and joy the cream filling?

Leader: How about leaving food out of the discussion, Schooner?

Schooner: Food makes me happy, boss.

Leader: Yes, I remember.

Schooner: But joy comes from knowing God!

Leader: *(hugs Schooner)* I'm glad you're paying attention.

Schooner: Joy, joy, joy, joy, joy.

Leader: Just saying the word makes you want to kick up your heels and dance, doesn't it?

Leader and Schooner: *(both move-to-the-groove of a silent joyful beat!)*

Leader: Today's Bible verse tells us to be joyful always.

Schooner: That sounds fabulous.

Leader: And pray always.

Schooner: Icing on the cake! *(sheepishly)* Sorry, boss.

Leader: And to give thanks in all circumstances. That means whatever the day brings—happiness, sadness, worries or fears—we are to be joyful and give thanks to God.

Schooner: Boy that's some l-o-n-g Bible Verse.

Leader: Not really. I added my two cents.

Schooner: I think your two cents makes lots of sense, boss.

Leader: Thank you, Schooner. Today's Bible story characters will have to hold on to God's joy with all their might.

Schooner: Why boss?

Leader: Because they're in prison.

Schooner: Oh, no. That's not a happy place.

Leader: But it becomes a place of joy because of the power of the Holy Spirit and the promises of God.

Schooner: Let's hurry on to Bible 4U! so I can hear the whole story. I'm ready to fly!

Leader: Joy coming on through—in Bible 4U! up next.

1 Bible 4U!

Welcome back to Bible 4U! Before we introduce today's story, I want you to think back to your younger days. Anyone ever play "London Bridge"? You know, "Take the keys and lock them up..." Invite kids to sing along, or even play a quick game if they're interested and time permits.

Well, our story is about two followers of Jesus who were locked up in prison. What was their crime? Good question! As Paul and Silas were telling people the good news about Jesus, they met a slave girl who could tell fortunes with the help of an evil spirit. In the name of Jesus, Paul and Silas commanded the spirit to leave the girl, and right away the girl was healed.

Instant Prep

Before class, ask three kids to play the roles of Davey, Rebecca and Dad. Give them copies of the "Jailbreak!" script below.

for Overachievers

Have a three-person drama team prepare the story. Create two sets: a Bibletime street scene and a simple home. Dress the kids in simple tunics. Create a faux leather Roman uniform for Dad.

Instead of being happy that the girl was healed, her owners were furious! Without the evil spirit, the girl couldn't earn money by telling fortunes. The girl's owners dragged Paul and Silas into the marketplace where they were beaten and sent to prison.

But prison walls didn't stop Paul and Silas. No, sir! They spread the joyful news of God's love to the whole prison, including the jailer and his family. Here come the jailer's two children now...

Jailbreak!
Based on Acts 16:16–19, 23, 25–34

Davey: Hi, I'm Davey and this is my kid sister, Rebecca.

Rebecca: *(loudly)* Davey! Davey! Look over there! There's that fortune telling slave girl.

Davey: *Sshh!* Do you want the other kids to see us? Don't you remember what happened last time?

Rebecca: *(sighing)* Oh, yeah. *(in a sing-song voice)* "Jailbirds, jailbirds, here come the jailbirds..."

Davey: Our dad *is* the head jailer here in Philippi.

Rebecca: I feel sorry for the girl, you know. She has some kind of evil spirit.

Davey: *(whispering)* There she is!

Rebecca: But look—she's not telling fortunes! She's following that Jewish preacher, Paul, the one who's been talking about Jesus. She looks different. I think that evil spirit is gone. She looks so happy!

Davey: I'll bet Paul got rid of her evil spirit. But her owners don't look at all happy. They're dragging Paul and his friend to the marketplace.

Rebecca: And a crowd is gathering…

Davey: *(Looks at Rebecca.)* If she can't tell fortunes, she's not going to make money for her owners. You know what that means…

Davey & Rebecca: FIGHT!

Kids cover their faces with their hands and watch the imaginary fight through spread fingers.

Davey: Come on, Becca. It's getting nasty here. Somebody's going to end up in jail. We'd better get home.

Rebecca: *(singing)* "Take the keys and lock them up, lock them up, lock them up! Take the keys and lock them up…"

Both kids walk away. They enter their home and sit down to dinner. Dad joins them.

Davey: Dad, we saw the fight that happened with that Paul guy. The crowd looked mad.

Dad: He got beaten pretty badly. I got orders to lock him up with extra security, so he and his friend are in the inner cellblock with their feet in stocks.

Rebecca: They must be miserable. I wish we could do something for them.

Davey: What did they do wrong?

Dad: Nothing except cast the demon out of that poor girl who used to tell fortunes.

Rebecca: But they were kind to her. I saw her. It's not fair that they're in jail.

Dad: I know. Maybe their God will help them.

Rebecca: I wish he would.

Dad: It's late. Get out your bedrolls. Let's get some sleep.

They lie down. Dad starts to snore immediately, then is wakened by singing offstage.

Davey: What's that? Somebody singing in the jail? It's the middle of the night!

Dad: It's Paul and Silas. When I locked them and chained them they were all beaten up, and now they're singing praises to their God. I've never heard anything like it.

Rebecca: How can they be joyful when such terrible things have happened to them?

Dad: I don't know, but…

All start shaking to simulate an earthquake.

Davey: Wh…what's that?

Dad: An earthquake! I've got to get to the jail! Whatever happens, stay here.

Davey and Rebecca grab onto each other and continue to shake while Dad staggers away.

Rebecca: What if the jail breaks apart and the prisoners get away?

Davey: Do you know how to pray?

Rebecca: No, but I think we should try.

They bow in prayer.

Davey: Dear God, we don't know much about you. We know that if you gave Paul the power to get rid of an evil spirit, you can protect our dad. Please keep him safe and don't let the prisoners get away. Amen.

Dad runs in.

Dad: The most wonderful has happened. The jail doors broke open in the earthquake and the chains fell off all the prisoners!

Rebecca: That's wonderful?

Dad: The wonderful part is that no one ran off! Paul and his friend Silas had everything under control. I was so thankful, I said, "Tell me what I need to do to be saved." And they told me about Jesus. Now they're coming over here to tell you, too. Davey, heat up some water so I can wash their wounds. Rebecca set some of last night's stew on the table. *They exit.*

Paul and Silas were so full of joy; they couldn't stop singing—even at midnight, even in prison. Their message of God's love brought joy to a dark, gloomy place. Let's talk a little bit more about that joy.

Toss the four numbered balls to different parts of the room. Bring the kids with the balls to the front one-by-one and ask these questions. Allow kids to get help from the group if they need it. After each correct answer, let kids drop their balls into a bag.

 ■ What made the prison a gloomy place? How did Paul and Silas change it to a joyful place?

 ■ It wasn't easy for Paul and Silas to be joyful in prison. When is it hard for you to be joyful?

 ■ How did the jailer and his family respond to the joyful message they heard from Paul and Silas?

 ■ How does knowing about God's love bring joy to your life?

Knowing about God's love transformed the jailer's life. After the earthquake, all the prison doors flew open. The prisoners' chains fell off, and they could have walked right out of the prison. When the jailer realized what had happened, he wanted to kill himself—because he knew he would be severely punished, or even killed for letting the prisoners escape. It was a sad, sad moment for the jailer.

Bible Verse
Be joyful always; pray continually; give thanks in all circumstances.
1 Thessalonians 5:16–18

But then Paul and Silas called out, "We are all here!" Not one of the prisoners had escaped! Right away, the jailer knew there was something special about these two men. The jailer invited Paul and Silas into his home, where they shared a meal and taught the jailer and his whole family about God's love. After listening to Paul and Silas, the jailer's whole family was filled with joy.

Joy comes from knowing God. Paul and Silas were joyful even in the worst possible circumstances. We can have that joy, too.

Today in your shepherd groups, you'll discover how to share the joy that comes from knowing God.

Dismiss kids to their shepherd groups.

② Shepherd's Spot

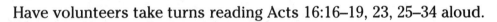

Gather your small group and help kids find Acts 16 in their Bibles.

You've probably heard the expression, "Out of the frying pan and into the fire." That's a good description of what happened with Paul and Silas and the other leaders of the early church. Spreading the Good News about Jesus and doing miracles to help those in need usually landed them in jail. As we read through the passage from the Bible, see if you can discover why things took such a nasty turn for Paul and Silas.

Have volunteers take turns reading Acts 16:16–19, 23, 25–34 aloud.

■ **What was Paul's big "crime"?**

■ **Did you ever get in trouble for doing something good? What was that like?**

One of the cool things we learn from this story is that no matter what happens, God's joy comes through. That's not something that we do for ourselves. It's a fruit of the spirit!

Pass out the "Jumpin' for Joy" handout. Have a volunteer read 1 Thessalonians 5:16–18 aloud: *"Be joyful always; pray continually; give thanks in all circumstances."*

■ **Paul and Silas were joyful—even when they were beaten and locked up in prison. How can you find that kind of joy?**

Have kids cut out the card and the word "JOY." Show them how to fold the card in half, cut the slits in the middle and pull the pop-up section forward. They may want to add bright colors or glitter glue edges to the word "JOY" before gluing it to the pop-up section. If you wish, let kids cut a piece of construction paper or gift wrap the same size as the card and glue it to the outside.

When the Holy Spirit is at work in our lives, God's joy pops out at the most unexpected times. Write a note of encouragement and pass the card on, or you may want to write your note of encouragement to yourself.

Invite kids to share prayer concerns. Then close with prayer. **Dear Lord, thank you for the incredible joy that comes from knowing you. Help us to know that no matter what happens to us, your joy is bubbling right below the surface. Today we bring to you our concerns for (mention kids' requests). Help us walk in your joy this week we pray, amen.**

Jumpin' for Joy

Make this fun pop-up to remind yourself or someone you care about that the spirit of God can fill you with joy no matter what's going on around you!

1. Cut out the card base and the JOY piece.

2. Fold the card base in half and clip the sides of the center section on the heavy lines. Pull the center section forward to make a pop-up base.

3. Glue the "JOY" piece to the pop-up.

If you wish, cut a piece of gift wrap the same size as the card base and glue it to the outside of the card.

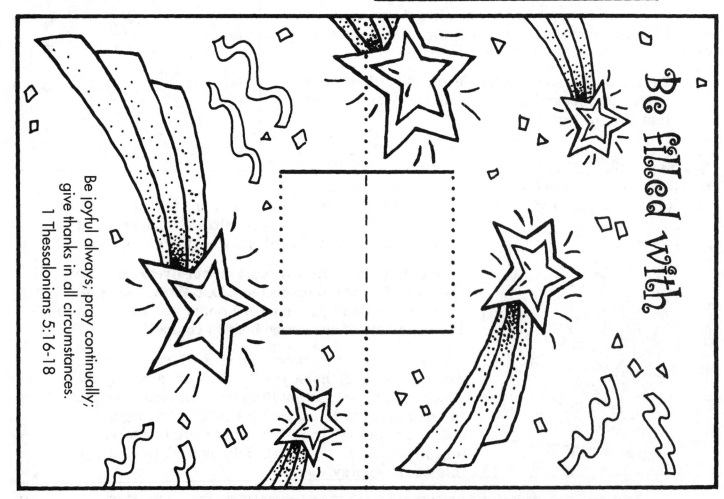

Be joyful always; pray continually; give thanks in all circumstances.
1 Thessalonians 5:16-18

Be filled with

Prisons are not happy places. With ankles fastened to wooden stocks and chains to keep wrists securely in place, Paul and Silas were in an unhappy spot with little to be joyful about.

Get List:
- ❑ thin licorice ropes or ribbon
- ❑ assorted mini-twist pretzels (plain, yogurt and chocolate dipped)

■ If you were chosen to bring one item of comfort to Paul and Silas what would that thing be?

■ Paul and Silas did not deserve prison time. What would your reaction be to such an unhappy place?

■ Having each other for company must have been a comfort for Paul and Silas. How is having loving friends a great comfort in times of worry and stress?

Despite their miserable circumstances, Paul and Silas filled the dark prison with joyful hymns of praise. That kind of joy comes from only one source—God himself! The Holy Spirit's encouraging voice whispers in our hearts that God is king over all the universe and he loves us and has not forgotten us. We're never alone or abandoned. God is closer than the next heartbeat. And that's something to be joyful about!

When an earthquake shook the prison, chains fell off and doors flew open. Paul and Silas saved the jailer's life by keeping everyone in their place. Any jailer who let his prisoners get away would be killed. The jailer was so grateful for Paul's help that he opened his heart to Christ. Joy filled his family as they were all baptized that night.

Let's make pretzel chains to remember that Paul and Silas sang of their joy in knowing God even when they were chained in prison. Let kids take licorice ropes and a handful of pretzels. Show them how to weave the licorice through the pretzel twists to form a chain.

Read 1 Thessalonians 5:16–18 aloud: *"Be joyful always; pray continually; give thanks in all circumstances."*

■ **What could "all circumstances" look like in your life this week?**

As we weave the licorice, notice how it goes up and down. Our lives have good times—the ups—and hard times—the downs. But God weaves his joy through everything that happens. Break a pretzel. **Bad times don't last forever. Neither do good times.** Hold up a licorice rope or length of ribbon. **Like a line that has no end, God's joy does last forever. The Holy Spirit weaves joy through everything that happens.**

Help kids tie chains to their wrists.

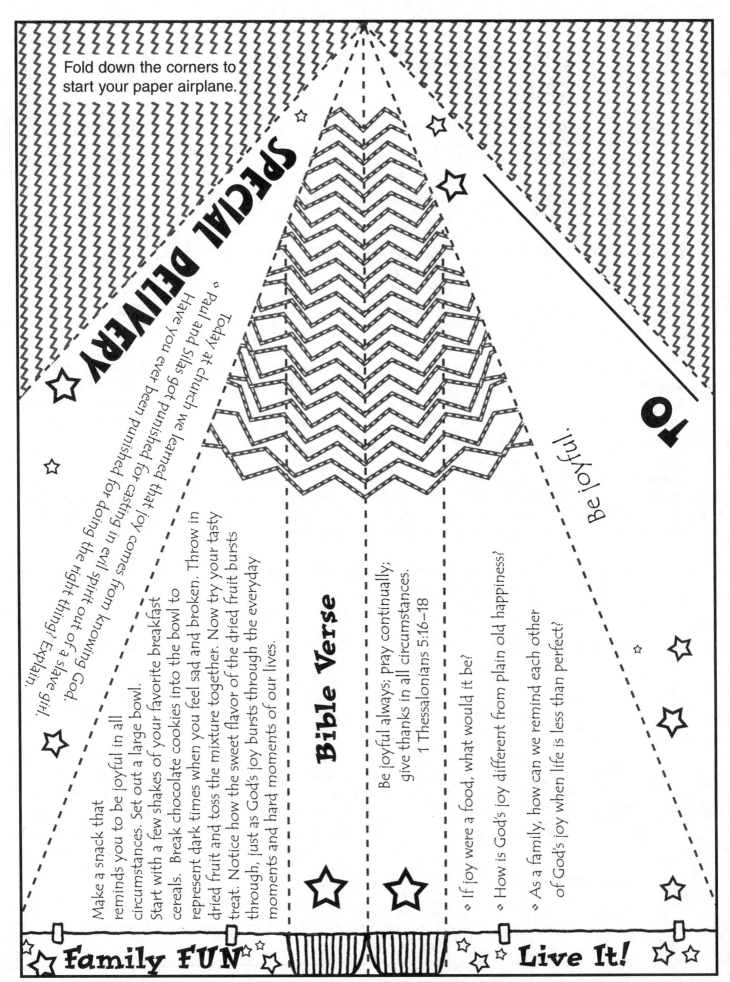

Fold down the corners to start your paper airplane.

SPECIAL DELIVERY

TO

Be joyful.

Today at church we learned that joy comes from knowing God. Paul and Silas got punished for casting in evil spirit out of a slave girl. Have you ever been punished for doing the right thing? Explain.

Make a snack that reminds you to be joyful in all circumstances. Set out a large bowl. Start with a few shakes of your favorite breakfast cereals. Break chocolate cookies into the bowl to represent dark times when you feel sad and broken. Throw in dried fruit and toss the mixture together. Now try your tasty treat. Notice how the sweet flavor of the dried fruit bursts through, just as God's joy bursts through the everyday moments and hard moments of our lives.

Bible Verse

Be joyful always; pray continually; give thanks in all circumstances.
1 Thessalonians 5:16–18

◇ If joy were a food, what would it be?

◇ How is God's joy different from plain old happiness?

◇ As a family, how can we remind each other of God's joy when life is less than perfect?

Family FUN

Live It!

The Chariot Chase

Option — Get Set
LARGE GROUP ■ Greet kids and do a puppet skit. Schooner learns the value of being patient.

❏ large bird puppet ❏ puppeteer

1 — Bible 4U! Instant Drama
LARGE GROUP ■ Introduce today's very active Bible story with this fun "Horsing Around" script.

❏ 4 actors ❏ copies of pp. 120-121, Horsing Around script ❏ 4 numbered balls
Optional: ❏ paper scroll ❏ two chairs ❏ rope ❏ a fancy robe and an ordinary Bibletime costume

2 — Shepherd's Spot
SMALL GROUP ■ Use the "Wrap Up" handout to create a keepsake of the good things the Holy Spirit creates in the lives of those who love Jesus.

❏ Bibles ❏ pencils ❏ scissors ❏ copies of p. 124, Wrap Up ❏ copies of p. 126, Special Delivery Optional: ❏ fruit flavored candies ❏ hole punch ❏ ribbon

Option — Workshop Wonders
SMALL GROUP ■ A variety of hand-tightened knots teaches a lesson on patience.

❏ Bibles ❏ clothesline cut into 18-inch lengths Optional ❏ teen helpers

Bible Basis
Philip and the Ethiopian.
Acts 8:4–6, 26–39

Learn It!
The Holy Spirit helps us teach others.

Live It!
Patiently share God's love.

Bible Verse
But the fruit of the Spirit is love, joy, peace, patience, kindness, goodness, faithfulness, gentleness and self-control. Galatians 5:22, 23.

Quick Takes

Acts 8:4–6, 26–39

8:4 Those who had been scattered preached the word wherever they went.
5 Philip went down to a city in Samaria and proclaimed the Christ there.
6 When the crowds heard Philip and saw the miraculous signs he did, they all paid close attention to what he said.
26 Now an angel of the Lord said to Philip, "Go south to the road—the desert road—that goes down from Jerusalem to Gaza."
27 So he started out, and on his way he met an Ethiopian eunuch, an important official in charge of all the treasury of Candace, queen of the Ethiopians. This man had gone to Jerusalem to worship,
28 and on his way home was sitting in his chariot reading the book of Isaiah the prophet.
29 The Spirit told Philip, "Go to that chariot and stay near it."
30 Then Philip ran up to the chariot and heard the man reading Isaiah the prophet. "Do you understand what you are reading?" Philip asked.
31 "How can I," he said, "unless someone explains it to me?" So he invited Philip to come up and sit with him.
32 The eunuch was reading this passage of Scripture: "He was led like a sheep to the slaughter, and as a lamb before the shearer is silent, so he did not open his mouth.
33 In his humiliation he was deprived of justice. Who can speak of his descendants? For his life was taken from the earth."
34 The eunuch asked Philip, "Tell me, please, who is the prophet talking about, himself or someone else?"
35 Then Philip began with that very passage of Scripture and told him the good news about Jesus.
36, 37 As they traveled along the road, they came to some water and the eunuch said, "Look, here is water. Why shouldn't I be baptized?"
38 And he gave orders to stop the chariot. Then both Philip and the eunuch went down into the water and Philip baptized him.
39 When they came up out of the water, the Spirit of the Lord suddenly took Philip away, and the eunuch did not see him again, but went on his way rejoicing.

Insights

As the systematic persecution of Christians made life in Jerusalem more difficult, groups of believers began a steady migration to outlying areas. And wherever the Christians went, they took the Gospel. So, as he often does, God used the negative—persecution—to bring about the positive, the timely spreading of the Gospel.

As Christians scattered from Jerusalem, an angel directed Philip to the region of Samaria. The city itself no longer existed—it was in ruins. But Philip found his target in a traveling Ethiopian official who was puzzling over the book of Isaiah. Running alongside the Ethiopian's chariot, Philip patiently waited for an opening. When the man wondered aloud how anyone could understand the scripture, Philip seized the opportunity and led the man to faith in Christ.

Wouldn't it be wonderful if our sharing Christ were always so quick to bear fruit? The Holy Spirit obviously sent Philip to the Ethiopian at just the right moment. As we share the Good News of Christ today, we may wait years to see people accept Christ. Use this lesson to encourage kids to listen patiently for direction from the Holy Spirit; then, when he says "Go," go!

Place a bandanna and a length of clothesline in Schooner's beak. Open with lively songs, then greet the kids. **I think there's a bird who's impatient to get started today. In fact…OUCH! He's pecking my ankle. Schooner…OUCH! Stop that! Come up here and tell me what you're so impatient about.** *Schooner pops up with the bandanna and rope in his beak.*

Schooner: *(muffled sound)* MmmMMMM.

Leader: What's that, Schooner?

Schooner: *(louder)* MmmMMMMmmMMMMM.

Leader: I can't understand what you're saying. Can I hold those things for you?

Schooner: *(nods his head "yes")*

Leader: *(takes the bandanna and rope)* How's that?

Schooner: *(exhales loudly)* Thank you.

Leader: What's up, besides my sore ankle?

Schooner: I can't tie my bandanna. And I've been trying and trying to throw a lasso. I can't do it and it's making me mad.

Leader: Getting mad won't help, you know.

Schooner: I know. I know. But I'm all thumbs with this.

Leader: I could say that I didn't know parrots had thumbs, but I can tell that this is no time for parrot jokes.

Schooner: You're such a sensitive guy, boss.

Leader: Maybe there's something I can do to help.

Schooner: You've got the bandanna. How about getting a move on?

Leader: But I don't have the most important thing. Your patience.

Schooner: *Squawk!* If patience is a supply I need, I'm all out!

Leader: Sound's like you need a little dose of fruit.

Schooner: Come again?

Leader: Patience is a fruit of the Spirit, Schooner.

Schooner: Oh. I'm feeling a little fruitless at the moment.

Leader: It's a good idea to practice patience in everything we do.

Schooner: That's pretty tough for me. I wish I could just hurry up and get patient.

Leader: God makes things happen in his time.

Schooner: What kinds of things?

Leader: Today we're going to hear about Philip who patiently ran beside a chariot so he could share God's love with someone.

Schooner: Can you run and be patient at the same time?

Leader: Sure can. When the time was right Philip was right there to tell a man about Jesus.

Schooner: I can't imagine a little parrot like me having that kind of patience.

Leader: Being patient is hard for most of us, Schooner. That's why the Holy Spirit helps us wait for things to happen in God's time.

Schooner: Speaking of help, are you ever going to help me get this bandanna tied? I don't want to be late for the barn dance.

Leader: I'd be glad to do the honors. *(ties the bandanna around Schooner's neck)*

Schooner: Now if I can just hurry up and learn to throw a lasso…

Leader: Schooner…

Schooner: Oops—I'm not being very patient, am I?

Leader: Learning to throw a lasso takes time.

Schooner: Maybe I can learn by next year's barn dance.

Leader: Now that's being a smart parrot.

Schooner: Would you mind putting that rope back in my beak?

Leader: It would be a pleasure. *(places the rope in Schooner's beak)* I hope you have a fun time. I'd like to see you do-si-do.

Schooner: *MMMmmmMMM.*

Leader: I think that's parrot talk for "Bible 4U! up next!" *Sqwauk!*

1 Bible 4U!

Timing is everything. God's timing is perfect. But waiting on God can sometimes take the patience of a saint. In today's story Philip perseveres when others may not have trusted God's leading, given up, gone home, and put their feet up.

Philip loved to tell others about Jesus. The church was just beginning and astonishing things were happening to the apostles. Miracles, lame people healed, evil spirits cast out, angels appearing to ordinary folks. It was during this time that the Holy Spirit directed Philip to the right place and moment to tell someone with a hungry heart about Jesus.

God used this encounter to spread the Gospel throughout Ethiopia. Imagine now a dusty road outside of Jerusalem. A chariot has just rumbled past, you listen to the clip clop of the horses' hooves echoing from a short distance ahead. As the clouds of dust begin to settle, you hear the sound of running feet. Give a listen now, as we hear the story, right from the horse's mouth, so to speak.

Horsing Around
Acts 8:4–6, 26–39

(Philip comes on stage running, then runs around the audience once. When he comes up front again he jogs in place and talks to them.)

PHILIP: Hi, I bet you're wondering why I am running. It may be hard to believe, but an angel told me to. *(runs around again and jogs in place at front)* My name is Philip, and I am a disciple of Jesus, the one who is the Christ. An angel told me to go to Gaza from Jerusalem, not an easy walk in itself. But on the way I saw that Ethiopian in the chariot over there *(points off stage left)* and the Spirit told me to stay near

him. I'm trying to catch up.

(He runs around again and as he does the Ethiopian enters stage right, trotting behind his two horses Mr. Ed and Charlie Horse. They stop center, in front of two chairs. Ethiopian sits, reading a scroll and horses jog in place. Philip trots up but does not say anything.)

Ethiopian: Wow, look at this. Hey, Mr. Ted, Charlie Horse, slow down a little. I want to read this scripture and you're bouncing too much. *(mime pulling back on reigns, horses slow to a walk)* This is prophecy written hundreds of years ago. Listen to this, "He was led like a sheep to the slaughter and as a lamb before the shearer is silent, so he did not open his mouth." What could that mean?

Mr. Ted: I don't know. *(pauses, then speaks louder)* I said I don't know! *(whinnies)* He's always asking us but he never seems to hear what we say!

Charlie Horse: He acts like he doesn't even understand. Hey, did you see that guy jogging behind us? He's been following us for miles. What's up with that? *(whinnies)*

Ethiopian: And listen to this: "In his humiliation he was deprived of justice. Who can speak of his descendants? For his life was taken from the earth."

Mr. Ted: Wow, that guy has finally caught up and he's still following us. Doesn't he ever give up?

Philip: Excuse me?

Ethiopian: Hello! Where did you come from?

Philip: I'm well, uh…. just jogging. Do you understand what you are reading?

Ethiopian: Tell me, please, who is the prophet talking about, himself or someone else?

Philip: Well…*(huff, huff)*…you see…*(huff, huff)*…

Charlie Horse: Why doesn't he let him into the chariot? Hey, let him get on. *(whinnies)*

Mr. Ted: He's going to have a heart attack. *(whinnies)*

Ethiopian: Why don't you get on board?

Philip: *(sits in other seat)* Phew! Thanks—just let me catch my breath.

Charlie Horse: I wonder how he just happened to be jogging here.

Mr. Ted: He seemed to be doing it on purpose. It took forever for our Master to see him

huffing and puffing back there. You'd think he would have dropped back long ago.

Philip: That scripture is talking about Jesus. He was crucified for no crime. He was silent as he faced his accusers. But he did it to take our place for the punishment for our sins.

Ethiopian: Tell me more.

(They mime talking while the horses talk.)

Charlie Horse: Do you think that's why he was following us? He knew that our Master would want an answer to his question?

Mr. Ted: How could he? If he did, he sure went to an awful lot of effort to make it happen.

Ethiopian: I believe you. I know in my heart what you've told me is true. Philip, look, there is some water. Why couldn't I be baptized right now? Whoa!

(He pulls on the reigns and they both jump out and run off stage left.)

Charlie Horse: Hey! Where are they going? I'd like a drink too.

Mr. Ted: Be patient, like Philip was. What are they doing? That's no way to get a drink. Is he trying to drown our Master?!

Charlie Horse: No, he's pulling him back out of the water. Wait a minute— did you see that?

Mr. Ted: What happened to Philip? He disappeared! He's gone!

(They both neigh worriedly.)

Ethiopian: *(enters stage left)* I'm a new person in Christ, Philip. Philip? *(looks around)* He's gone! How strange—it's almost as if God took him away. Come on Charlie and Mr. Ted, let's get you a drink and get back to town so I can tell everyone about my faith in Jesus.

(He leads them off stage.)

I wonder if Philip had good running shoes? He did have a never-give-up attitude that he used for God. The Ethiopian must have been very surprised to have his questions answered right when he needed it. The Ethiopian went home to tell everyone he knew about what had happened to him. God multiplied what Philip did many times over.

Toss the four numbered balls to different parts of the room. Bring kids with the balls to the front one-by-one and ask these questions. Allow kids to get help from the group if they need it. After each correct answer, let kids drop their balls into a bag.

 ■ **Why did Philip decide to go to Gaza?**

 ■ **What was the Ethiopian reading in the chariot?**

 ■ **What would have happened if Philip had given up too soon?**

 ■ **Why is patience important when we're telling others about God's love?**

Instant rice, microwave popcorn and hurry-up self-serve lines at the grocery stores show what impatient people we are. We want things to happen right now! Here's something very important for you to remember: telling others about Jesus is not a rush job! The Holy Spirit prepares the heart of the listener and the one who's sharing.

Who knows how long the Ethiopian in today's story had read the Scriptures? The Holy Spirit sent Philip at just the right time, and Philip waited patiently to answer the man's questions. The Holy Spirit gives us patience when we remember that God's time is always the right time.

Bible Verse
But the fruit of the Spirit is love, joy, peace, patience, kind-ness, goodness, faithfulness, gentleness and self-control.
Galatians 5:22, 23

Today in your shepherd groups you'll see how much you can remember about the fruit of the spirit.

Dismiss kids to their shepherd groups.

Gather your small group and help kids find Acts 8 in their Bibles.

Did you ever have to wait and wait and wait to get someone's attention? You might clear your throat, or wave your hand wildly to your teacher. Then *finally*, finally, the other person takes notice. That's exactly what happened to Philip, except while he was waiting to be noticed he was running alongside a chariot. That leaves me out of breath, how about you? Maybe we have just enough breath left to read the Bible story.

Have volunteers take turns reading Acts 8:4–6, 26–39 aloud.

■ **How did the Holy Spirit direct Philip in this story?**

■ **How did Philip's patience pay off?**

For the past several weeks we've been learning a lot about the fruit of the spirit. Patience is the last addition to our collection. Let's see if we can name the fruit of the spirit. *(Love, joy, peace, patience, kindness, goodness, gentleness, faithfulness, self-control.)*

■ **We also talked about other things the Holy Spirit does for those who love Jesus. Who remembers some of those things?** *(He never leaves us alone, he is our counselor, he gives us power to do God's work, he gives us courage to speak out for Jesus.)*

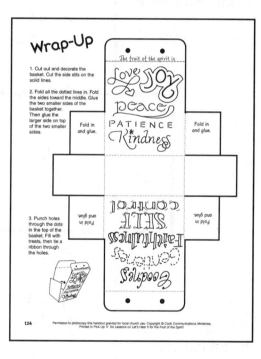

You've learned so much! Let's bag it up so you can take it with you! Distribute the "Wrap Up" handout. Show kids how to cut out the bag and fold in on the dotted lines. A bit of glue on the tabs will hold the bag together. If you wish let kids take a handful of fruit-flavored candy to fill their bags. Tie the bags with colorful ribbon.

■ **As we've studied the fruit of the spirit, how have you seen God work in your life?**

■ **Which fruit would you like to ask God to give you more of?**

We can try hard to make these things happen on our own, but it's the Holy Spirit who truly changes us from the inside out!

Invite kids to share prayer concerns, then close with prayer. **Dear Heavenly Father, thank you for sending your spirit to be our friend and counselor who's with us every day. Keep our hearts in tune with you so that this wonderful fruit will grow in our lives. Please hear our prayers for** (mention kids' concerns). **In Jesus' name, amen.**

Wrap-Up

1. Cut out and decorate the basket. Cut the side slits on the solid lines.

2. Fold all the dotted lines in. Fold the sides toward the middle. Glue the two smaller sides of the basket together. Then glue the larger side on top of the two smaller sides.

3. Punch holes through the dots in the top of the basket. Fill with treats, then tie a ribbon through the holes.

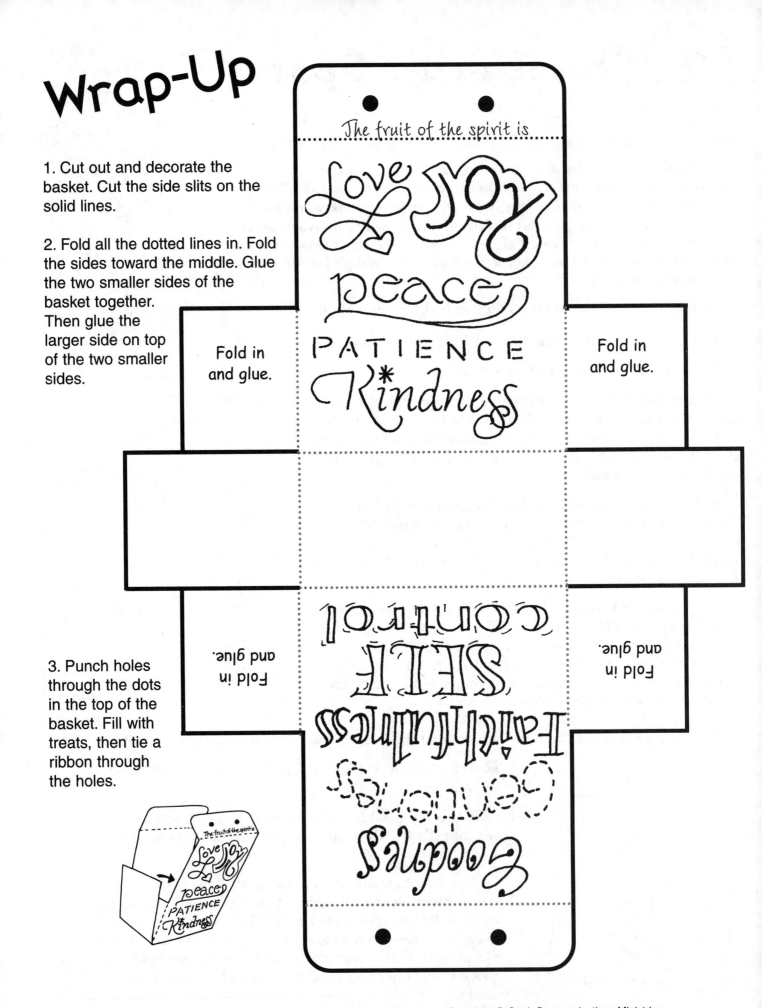

The fruit of the spirit is

Love Joy peace PATIENCE *Kindness

Fold in and glue.

Fold in and glue.

Fold in and glue.

Fold in and glue.

SELF control Faithfulness Gentleness Goodness

Workshop Wonders

Gather your kids and have them form two groups.

Today we learned something about patience. When God sent Philip to Samaria, he patiently ran beside the Ethiopian man's chariot until the man was ready to hear about Jesus.

■ **When do you find it hardest to be patient?**

Did you ever need to explain something really important, but the person you were telling just didn't get it? Sometimes it takes a lot of patience to help someone understand who Jesus is and how he can become our Savior.

Let's see if you can learn a handy skill, then patiently teach it to someone in the other group.

Each group will learn to tie a different knot. After you've learned your knot, find someone from the other "knot" group. Take a few minutes and patiently teach each other your knots. Then you'll know two!

Get List:
- Bibles
- clothesline cut into 18-inch lengths
- photocopies of knot tying diagrams

Optional
- teen helpers

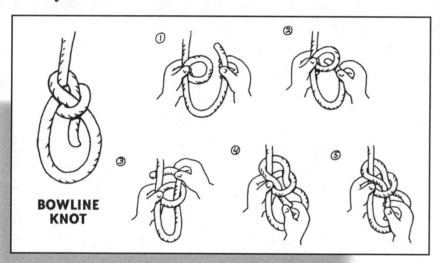

BOWLINE KNOT

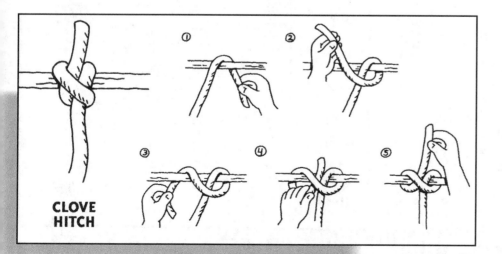

CLOVE HITCH

Give each student an 18-inch length of clothesline. Have a teen or adult helper assist kids with learning the knots by following the diagrams below. Kids working on the clove hitch knot will need table or chair legs to work with. After everyone has learned and shared a knot, bring the groups back together. Debrief the activity with the following questions:

■ **What can you learn from this experience that will help you share God's love with other people?** *(Be patient; say things in a way that people will understand.)*

■ **Why should we remember that the Holy Spirit helps us teach others?** *(He helps us know what to say; because we know he can help us.)*

Fold down the corners to start your paper airplane.

SPECIAL DELIVERY

TO

Patiently share God's love.

Today at church we learned to patiently share God's love. What highlights do you remember from today's story about Philip and the Ethiopian that you can share with your parents? Name some of the best times to tell others about Jesus.

Bible Verse

But the fruit of the spirit is love, joy, peace, patience, kindness, goodness, faithfulness, gentleness and self-control. Galatians 5:22, 23

Is patience impossible for you? Let the Holy Spirit help. Perform this little experiment and see the impossible—watch it rain under water! Fill a glass with water. Take the open end of a balloon and push in two marbles for weight. Fill the balloon with warm water and a few drops of blue food coloring. Squeeze the balloon nozzle and drop it into the water glass. Release. Watch patiently as blue water rises then rains down the inside of the glass!

◊ What is the absolutely, hands-down, toughest time for you to be patient?
◊ Talk about the fruit of the spirit—how do you see it demonstrated in your family?
◊ Pick a night to have a "fruit check." Make fruit slushies in a blender, then tell how you've seen the fruit of the spirit in each other's lives.

☆ **Family FUN** ☆

Live It!

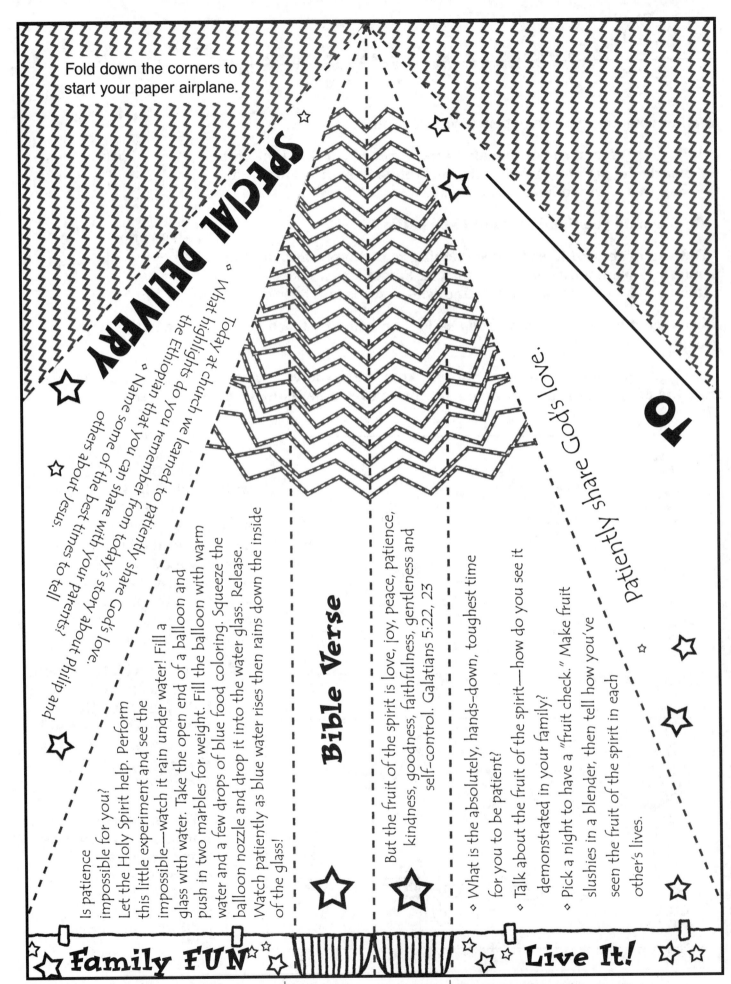